Please return or renew this item before the latest date shown below

KY

Renewals can be made
by internet   www.fifedirect.org.uk/libraries
in person   at any library in Fife
by phone   08451 55 00 66

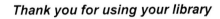

Thank you for using your library

Open Books
PRESS

Published by Open Books Press, USA
www.openbookspress.com

An imprint of Pen & Publish, Inc.
Bloomington, Indiana
(812) 837-9226
info@PenandPublish.com

www.PenandPublish.com

ISBN: 978-0-9852737-1-2
LCCN: 2011943804

This book is printed on acid free paper.

Printed in the USA

INTRODUCTION

He looked almost lifelike in his dark blue Pierre Cardin suit with the burgundy pinstripes, the one he liked to wear for all the special occasions. The matching burgundy Hugo Boss tie was knotted perfectly below the starched white collar of his clean white shirt. Hundreds of roses, mostly whites, yellows and reds, surrounded his open casket, as a video of his life in streaming still photographs played on three screens high above his head.

Men in designer suits similar to his and women in stylish hats with black lace veils filed into the Abyssinian Baptist Church and walked slowly down the long incline of the sanctuary for that one last chance to touch his clasped hands, pray silently, whisper farewell, and maybe even plant a soft kiss on his forehead. By the time Rev. Kevin R. Johnson was calling him "a brother, son, colleague, a soldier in the courtroom, a voice for the voiceless, and a savior of many," the church was filled to capacity and there was gridlock outside from the double-parked cars and limousines on Odell Park Place in Harlem.

A slight, be-speckled black man in grease-stained clothing gazed at the long line of automobiles outside the church and smiled, seemingly to himself. Then, looking at no one in particular, he drew a deep breath and shouted out, "Man, oh man, it's great to be alive, isn't it?"

The irony of the man's rhetoric surely would not have been lost on Robert Dunn. It was a glorious day for the day after Memorial Day: temperatures in the 70s, tolerable humidity, and the Yankees about to start a three-game series in Kansas City. Robert no doubt would have looked at that man outside the church, and he would have seen past his obvious drunkenness and probable homelessness to his wisdom and his timing and his unconscious ability to play the role of the street-corner philosopher. Robert probably would have given the man some money, perhaps even counseling him about his life during the transaction. At a certain point, though, Robert would have looked at his watch and realized that he needed to get home. The Yankees would soon be coming to bat in the top of the first.

What Robert would never know, of course, was how woeful the Bronx Bombers looked in Kansas City that week, losing all three games to the Royals, a humiliating sweep that was followed by two of three losses in Minnesota, then another two of three losses in Milwaukee, and then amazingly another two of three losses in St. Louis. If only Robert could have spoken from wherever his soul went, he might have reasoned how better off he was missing that horrible road trip. Robert hated losing. He was a winner, a hero to the hundreds crammed inside the church; at times their spokesman, and always their champion. But on that day after Memorial Day the time had come for them to speak about him. And so they came to the pulpit offering eulogies and testament as to what he had come to mean in their lives.

Rev. Rose McCray, a childhood friend, spoke of how he had motivated her to apply to Harvard, and then to graduate school later on. "Bobby lived large," she said. "He told me that anything is possible. He was an awesome man who blessed us with every ounce of his presence."

Judge Leslie Crocker Snyder said that no trial attorney ever dared talk to her in open court quite like Robert. "I overruled one of his suggestions," she recalled, "and he started yelling at me, telling me, 'You can't do that.' Then he apologized for the outburst and said it would never happen again. Of course, that was a lie because it happened all the time. He delivered some of the best cross-examinations I've ever heard. But he also took advantage of my feelings for him. He could sweet-talk anyone."

His cousin Kent Dunn told of how Robert had rushed into a burning house when he was a pre-teen and found six children, all under the age of seven, huddled together in one of the rooms. "Their mother had left these kids alone," Kent Dunn said, "and Bobby carried them all out to safety. He even had the presence of mind to turn off the gas in the kitchen." Kent Dunn called his cousin's heroics, "the defining moment of his life."

Many among the sea of black faces who had known Robert Dunn since childhood nodded approvingly at the recollection. But for another family, the family of white people seated down front in a church pew directly behind Robert's own next of kin, it was the more recent events of his life that mattered most. Unlike practically everyone else in the church, these white people only knew Robert for a short time, and yet they were privy to classified information that had not yet been provided to the others. If the majority of mourners had been aware of this information, they would have rightly concluded that the real defining moment of Robert's life was not the selfless act of a pre-teen but rather the powerful, complex and racially-charged set of circumstances that preceded his death. *Change of Heart* is the story of those circumstances, and how one man's decision to confront his darkest fears and twisted beliefs made it possible for him to find the most unique kind of unconditional love, a love that could only be experienced from the inside out.

CHAPTER ONE

The long line of two-family aluminum-sided cream-colored houses on 112th Rd., in the St. Albans section of Queens, had the monotonous feel of civilian quarters on a military base. Separated only by narrow driveways, thin hedgerows, and tiny fenced-in front yards made of dirt and trampled-down grass, it sometimes came down to the three-wheeler bikes outside and the muted tones of the living-room drapes that kept people from walking into the wrong house at the wrong time.

Robert Dunn's earliest memories go back to one of those houses, where he lived in the late-1950s with his older sister Sharon, and their parents, Robert Sr., and Dolores. "It seemed everyone on the block lived cookie-cutter lives," Robert recalled of his childhood. "Most of the men usually left for work at the same time each morning. Most of their wives stayed home. Children attended either the local public or Catholic school and spent their evenings in the street, playing stick ball, punch ball, or skelly, which involved flicking bottle tops. Everyone on the block ate dinner at the same time, and because the houses were so close, we could hear our neighbors washing their dishes."

But there was one big difference about the Dunn family that set them far apart from the other families on the block: They were black, and everyone else was white.

Being the first black family to move into a predominantly Irish-Catholic neighborhood never felt like a badge of honor to Robert's father, like something he had to hold up as a source of pride. He was happy enough just blending in and providing for his family like the other hard-working men in the neighborhood. Robert Sr. worked in those years for a man named Jack Allen, a local merchant who started in business selling carpet remnants on the sidewalks along Jamaica Avenue, and then door-to-door, until he had enough money to open his own shop. That shop, Allen Carpet, went on to become one of the most successful carpet chains in the country, and in the process, Jack Allen and his brothers became millionaires.

Unfortunately for Robert Sr., the wealth never trickled down. A few hundred times a day, Dunn would haul the carpets through the store, unroll them to show the customers, and then roll them back up and put them away. He did earn the boss's respect and eventually he became Jack Allen's right-hand man. But both men knew there was a glass ceiling that Dunn would never break through.

"God, Robbie," Allen would say to him, "if only you were white, I'd make you a partner."

Jack Allen did find other ways to compensate his loyal worker by helping him out from time to time providing jobs for his relatives. But it was clear from the outset that Dunn would never get rich in the carpet business. He did pocket some extra cash by occasionally selling carpet from the back of the truck that Allen allowed him to drive home, but he excused the behavior as an entitlement, something he deserved. After all, he had worked his ass off during the day, so why not make a few extra dollars at night? It seemed perfectly reasonable to him, even if he wasn't disclosing the additional income to the Internal Revenue Service.

"My father had learned to live life by not straying too far outside the margins," was how his son remembered it.

Robert's father also found significant support in alcohol. Like so many others before and after him, he drank to escape the pressures of work and his responsibilities at home. An absentee father, he would often come home at 4 a.m., reeking of booze and demanding that his wife get out of bed to cook him dinner. "I can still remember my mother's shrillness as she upbraided him," said their son. "She wound up pushing him further and further away in order to protect us."

But to the outside world, and even to their extended family members, Dolores kept a stoic front. She'd be out with her young son Robert, and people she knew would politely ask, "How are you?"

And Dolores' answer was always the obligatory simple word, "Fine."

Although they weren't exactly her son's first words, as soon as he heard his mother say "fine," he got right in her face to challenge her. "If you are fine," he would say, "then how come you and daddy are fighting all the time?"

Robert wasn't yet three when his parents separated. Dolores Dunn and her two young children remained in the house on 112th Rd., and Robert Dunn Sr. moved into his mother's house nearby. A similar two-family house, with his grandparents living downstairs and his aunt, uncle and two cousins on the top floor, Robert at least felt welcomed by his grandparents and the rest of the family.

But it was his father, more than anyone, who didn't have a clue as to how to deal with his young son. When he wasn't drinking, Robert Sr. was a quiet and withdrawn individual, especially around his family. "You would never know my father was so haunted by demons unless you were there to witness his behavior after a few drinks," Robert said, looking back. "It was then that his hostility came to the surface, and it became obvious to me that my father didn't care to be around me."

"My father didn't know how to deal with Bobby's hyperactivity," Sharon Dunn recalled. "And for Bobby it was the first in a long line of rejections. Bobby was always loveable, but he gave the appearance of being wild and unruly. Today they would call it Attention Deficit Hyperactivity Disorder, or ADHD. And for my brother it definitely went un-diagnosed."

But the rest of the family took a lot of interest in the Dunn children, Robert recalled, "Because we were from a broken home. Theirs was a house of intact families. We'd walk from church, and my grandmother would make us say hello to everyone we passed. 'Howdy Doo' to everyone. Not just hello. It had to be more. 'How do you do?' Or, 'Howdy Doo.'

"My sister would say, 'Nana, we don't say that.'

"And grandmother would say, 'Oh, but you will say it today.'"

As young Robert shuttled back and forth between houses, it didn't take him long to realize that there were many more black families living on his grandmother's block, and how differently he was being treated from one street to the next.

"From the time I started going out on the street in front of my mother's house, none of the kids wanted to play with me," he said. "I'd hear them say, 'Don't play with that tar baby' or 'that crispy critter,' or 'that nigger.' I'd go back to my mother and ask her, 'Why are they saying that?' and, of course, she'd try to explain it as best she could, telling me not to pay them any mind. But it still confused me, and made me very angry."

Robert tried his best to gain acceptance from the other children. He would often take his mother's jewelry or coins from her pockets and give it to kids in the neighborhood, trying in a way to buy them. But it rarely worked, and as Robert got older he began to understand why. He was the black kid, and if he wanted to play anywhere beyond the few feet of sidewalk in front of his house, he did so at his own peril. His mother even tried to protect him by making him wear a harness attached to the backyard clothesline, to keep him from straying. Ultimately that didn't work either.

One summer evening when Robert was an adventurous six-year-old, as the neighborhood glowed under the soft reddish hue of dusk, he grabbed the toy air gun he'd received the previous Christmas and walked around the corner to a construction site on 196th St. Three houses were being built on the site. They were larger than the ones on his block, and with the workers having gone for the night there was plenty of room for him to crawl around the dirt, shooting his air gun at imaginary Nazis and gunslingers from the Old West. He was just a kid in his own fantasy world, blasting away at targets that weren't there, and never noticing for one second that five older white kids had crept up behind him. The trance was broken when they suddenly began pelting him with dirt and rocks.

"You little nigger," one said. "What are you doing here?"

Robert dropped his air gun, grabbed a few rocks of his own, and began throwing back at his twelve-year-old tormentors. "I was outnumbered," he said, "and as they closed in, I took off into a half-built house and scampered up a wooden staircase to an open landing on the second floor.

The white boys chased me inside and cornered me. A few climbed an exterior wall to get me—they didn't even bother taking the staircase," he said. "I promised them that if they let me go, I'd go straight home."

"You're not going anywhere, spook," one boy said.

Robert couldn't recall which boy threw the first punch. "All I remember is trying to fight back despite the odds against me," he said. "They were on top of me, hitting me and kicking me repeatedly. Then one of the boys said, 'Let's throw him.'

They grabbed me by the arms and legs and swung me back and forth," he said. "The whole side of the house was open—no windows anywhere, just open space. They swung me once, twice, and on the third swing they let go. I flew out of the open house into the warm night air, and landed in the basement area, two stories down, on a soft pile of excavated dirt. I can't actually recall if I lost consciousness when I hit the ground, but I definitely had the wind knocked out of me. As I lay there, motionless, I could see one of the kids looking down on me from the landing. I think they were afraid, and they took off."

Two weeks later, Robert's sister Sharon was on her way home from Betty's Laundromat, pushing a cart of folded laundry—the Dunns had a washing machine in the house, but no dryer. As she passed the same construction site, a group of older white kids stopped her and pulled her into one of the unfinished houses. They felt her breasts and pulled her clothes off, trying to get her panties down. She screamed and cried and tried her best to fight back until, finally, they let her go. She wasn't raped, but she came home crying. Robert was too young to understand the sexual connotations of the attack, but neither child ever set foot near that construction site again.

That fall, Robert's mother enrolled her son in the first grade at St. Pascal Babylon, a Catholic school just a few blocks from home. Most of the black kids in St. Albans went to public school, but Dolores thought her two children would receive a better education in more regimented surroundings. Sharon was a much easier child, and she thrived at St. Pascal, never feeling isolated or singled out.

"But I might as well have gone to school with a bull's eye on my back," said Robert. "I was hyperactive and hadn't gone to kindergarten, so by the time I entered first grade, I was unruly, undisciplined, and unfamiliar with behaving in a controlled environment."

There were other African-American kids at St. Pascal, and as more and more of them enrolled in the 1960s, their presence seemed to become a threat. "The nuns had determined that we were a breed apart—people who were raised differently, presumably more prone to violence in reaction to authority," said Robert. "They felt they had to crack down on us, to teach us who was boss.

So the nuns would beat the crap out of me," he said. "And I'm not talking about a whack on the hand with a ruler. Once four nuns shoved me into the broom closet, and all four of them took turns hitting me. I remember it clearly. The room was dark, with wooden shutters on the doors—little slats that let in tiny rays of light. The nuns kneed me. They pushed me back and forth, saying, 'We'll show you.'

"I had nightmares for years of these white hands catching light through the slats—chalky hands that wrote with chalk and never wore nail polish," he said, "menacing hands with crooked fingers."

When the school year ended, Dolores turned her two children over to the Fresh Air Fund, the independent nonprofit agency that had been providing summer vacations to inner city youth since 1877. Sharon was sent to live with a family in Chappaqua, a burgeoning upper middle class community in northern Westchester County. On her first day there, her host family threw a party at one of the community swimming pools in the area, and they invited all the neighborhood kids and their mothers, who came with beach bags full of towels, swimming trunks, snorkels, and water wings.

Sharon wasn't much of a swimmer, but she jumped right into the pool. As she began flailing around in the water, some of the mothers panicked, yelling at their children to get out of the pool, yanking their skinny arms to pull them away from Sharon.

"My child is not getting back into the pool until it's drained and cleaned," one mother snapped at the host. Other hysterical mothers agreed. Sharon asked if she could use the phone to call home, and she was back in Queens by the next day. The experience devastated her.

The same day Sharon left for Chappaqua Robert boarded a train and was told he was going to Pennsylvania. No representative of the Fresh Air Fund, and not even his mother realized that the identification tag around Robert's neck had been improperly filled out. When other kids got off the train in Pennsylvania, he was told to stay aboard. Four other boys also had the wrong tags, and the five of them ended up in Virginia.

The train platform in Virginia was crowded with white families picking up black children with correct tags. As the organizers herded kids to their assigned destinations, someone in authority suddenly realized that five boys had no place to go.

"We became like slaves on an auction block, standing side by side on an elevated platform and waiting for someone—anyone—to take us," said Robert. "I was just a kid, but I can still remember the man holding his hand over my head and shouting, 'Okay, who wants this one?'"

A woman whose friend was picking up another child spoke up. "I'll take him."

"My mother had no idea I wasn't in Pennsylvania, much less in Virginia with a woman who had no connection at all to the Fresh Air Fund," said Robert. "Too young to realize that I should be frightened, I was just grateful that someone, anyone, was feeding me and showing me to a room. But that night, after I was already in bed, the woman's husband came home, and I heard a muffled argument erupt. Then the man came storming into my room, switched on the light, stared at me, and screamed back to his wife, 'You said he was a spic. He's a nigger. You don't know the difference between a spic and a nigger? He's a nigger.'"

The woman was so petrified by her husband's reaction that she found another home for Robert the next day. The home turned out to be a farm, also in Virginia, which was run by another white woman and her fifteen-year-old nephew. They already had six black children living there. Robert Dunn became the seventh.

But this wasn't the relaxing rural experience he was expecting. "The woman and her nephew used us to care for their animals and tend their fields," he said. "I remember how the nephew broke a branch from a tree and whittled it until it was thin enough to crack in the air over our heads. That was his way of keeping us in line."

And the living conditions on the farm were no better, as the seven boys had to share one outhouse and had no access to running water or plumbing. Instead, there was a tub on one corner of the roof that collected rainwater. To shower, one of the boys had to stand under the tub, while another boy, up on the roof, tipped the tub to pour the water on him, while the white woman scrubbed him with a hard brush. "Let me get the dirt and some of that black off you," she'd say. "Boy, by the time you go home, you'll be three shades lighter."

"For three weeks, I endured the woman's scrubbings, her nephew's taunts, and unpaid servitude on the farm. Then I returned home to a neighborhood in transition," said Robert, happy to recall the thought of being back in his own environment. "As black families moved into the neighborhood, white families moved out. Within a few years, blacks were the majority on our block, and as our numbers increased, so did the tension between the races. Soon there were constant racial brawls, with cousins and older brothers from both sides coming into the neighborhood to battle.

In 1966, when I was eleven," he said, "the nuns at St. Pascal expelled me from school. My mother didn't want to send me to the public school in St. Albans, so she sold the house in Queens, gave some of the proceeds to my father, and used the rest of the money to buy a house in Roosevelt, Long Island. By then, my attitude about whites was solidified: they were the enemy."

CHAPTER TWO

In 1939, Helen Doherty and her three-year-old daughter Betty were riding through their predominantly Irish-Catholic neighborhood in the Bronx, off on a trip down to the Central Park Zoo in Manhattan, when the bus suddenly struck a steel pillar underneath an elevated subway platform.

There was some jostling inside the bus, and more than a few gasps, but amazingly no one was hurt even a little. Still, the bus driver insisted that everyone remain seated in place so he could check the exterior of the bus and then find the nearest policeman.

Although it would take the New York City Transit Authority another forty-four years just to begin the process of outfitting its buses with air-conditioners, the passengers that day in 1939 didn't become openly hostile as the temperature inside the bus began to climb. Of course, that didn't stop some of them from eyeing one another, almost suspiciously, as New Yorkers are often prone to do during a surprise communal experience, as though the accident might have been caused by the pillar, or another motorist, or maybe even someone on the bus other than the driver.

Like any curious three-year-old, Betty looked around too. The men in their suits and ties and dark narrow-brim hats and the women in their floral dresses and made-up lips looked mostly like the kind of people Betty had observed since infancy—white, working-class urbanites who always dressed for success when venturing downtown, whether they were on their way to work, or to Radio City Music Hall to see a big Hollywood movie and a spectacular stage show, or even on their way to the zoo to feed the animals and eat some cotton candy.

And then Betty saw him, the one man on the bus who looked nothing like his fellow-travelers. This man was definitely African-American, and he was staring directly at Betty. He was probably the first black person she ever saw up close, and the very idea that he was looking in her direction frightened her.

But she couldn't turn away either, and as he held her gaze, beads of sweat dripping down his face in the intolerable heat, Betty shrank closer to her mother, even more terrified. Sensing her little girl's upset, Helen Doherty wrapped her arms around her little girl, pulled her tight, and whispered in her tiny ear, "You never have to be afraid of a black person. His heart is as red as yours."

Betty never forgot her mother's reassuring words, and many, many years later no one would live to appreciate that more than Robert Dunn.

Helen Doherty, a stately woman with deep-set green eyes and the thin, angular face of a fashion model, may have known instinctively how to protect her children while teaching them racial tolerance, but she could not ultimately protect herself from infectious disease, and in 1940, barely a year after that harmless bus accident in the Bronx, she died of tuberculosis, leaving her husband, William, as sole care of their three children: four-year-old Betty, her nine-year-old sister Helen, and their three-year-old brother, Billy Jr.

Parenting was not something that came easily to William Doherty, an Irish immigrant and a skilled laborer who became a New York City subway repairman and then took on a second job working at night in a lipstick factory when it became apparent that the war raging in Europe would sooner or later involve the United States. Even at four, Betty knew how hard her father was working just to provide for his family, and she even managed to figure out a way to help him.

"People would become very charitable on holidays like Thanksgiving and Christmas, and I remember that Thanksgiving walking alone up to the Grand Concourse," Betty said of the expansive Bronx thoroughfare, "and asking for charity, with my hand out. Some people did give me money, and when I gave the money to my father and told him I got it asking for charity on the Grand Concourse, he cracked me across my face. He was a very proud man, and the thought that his baby daughter was begging for money in the neighborhood embarrassed him, and devastated him."

In fact, William Doherty needed significantly more money than his youngest daughter could ever collect, and it didn't take long before the strain of two jobs, coupled with single parenthood and heavy drinking, became much too much for him to handle. One night he gathered his three children together and told them they'd all been exposed to tuberculosis, the disease that had taken their mother. He said that because TB had grown to epidemic proportions, resulting in thousands of deaths, perhaps the kids would be better off living in a more rural setting. Betty took that to mean the family was moving, and she remembered feeling excited by the prospect of this new adventure.

But the kind of adventure Betty was anticipating was hardly the plan that her father had set in motion. For starters, he wasn't moving anywhere. And the rural setting he chose for his children turned out not to be a new house but St. Agatha's, a Catholic orphanage in Nanuet, NY.

The rural life that Betty had conjured up in her young mind certainly existed in Nanuet, but most of it could be found outside the gates of the orphanage, a large compound made up red dorms, white dorms, outhouses and one immense four-story-high church. St. Agatha's was home to children of all ages, and the nuns decided which kids would be housed in which dorms depending on their age and the state of their health. Because the three Doherty children had a mother who died of tuberculosis, they were assigned to a white building that everyone there referred to as "The Preview."

The building, like the hospital facility on the South side of Ellis Island, where immigrants with health issues were detained prior to being granted permission to enter the United States, was a sort of way station for those children who needed medical supervision prior to joining the larger orphanage population in other dorm buildings. And while Betty and her siblings were neither sick nor showing any signs that they might actually become sick, they were sent to The Preview as a precaution because they had once been exposed to their mother's fatal illness.

"I didn't know it at the time, but we were quarantined," recalled Betty. "The nuns took my sister Helen off to be with older girls. Billy was brought to a room where only the sick baby boys lived. And I was left to be with girls my own age. We were kept in The Preview for three months. I was afraid, but like I proved to myself when I went up to the Grand Concourse looking for charity, I wasn't afraid to take chances."

She remembered once stealing bread from The Preview kitchen and taking it to her baby brother's room. "I think in my head I was rebelling," she said. "It was a strict, regimented existence. The nuns even cancelled Christmas that year because we were bad. Nobody got any presents."

Her father didn't bring presents that Christmas either. And soon he stopped coming altogether. Betty longed to go home, but she was too young to know that her father's drinking had escalated to such a crisis point that one night he actually hauled all the furniture out of his apartment and dumped it into the Hudson River. His three kids had no way of knowing it at the time, but they would remain at St. Agatha's for years. St. Agatha's was where they grew up. The orphanage became their home.

Betty Doherty would live at St. Agatha's for thirteen years, from 1940-1953. Like others from the orphanage, when she was old enough to start attending school, she would get on a school bus each day and go to one of the public schools in the area. When she was old enough to start working, she got a job cleaning people's homes in Nanuet. She was still living in the orphanage during her teenage years, still taking the bus to Pearl River High School, and doing her homework like all the other kids. Only she wasn't like all the other kids.

"They always called us 'The Home Kids' because we came from an orphanage," she said. "It wasn't pleasant to hear. I couldn't wait to find a life for myself outside of that place."

The opportunity came in 1953 when Betty boarded a bus in Nanuet that was bound for New York City. Betty was only taking the bus as far as Pearl River, and when she stepped off at her stop she landed funny on the pavement and badly twisted her knee. She called her sister Helen, who was now married and living in Manhattan. Betty knew she needed to go to the hospital, and the two sisters realized that if she returned to St. Agatha's she risked winding up again, many years later, in The Preview.

"I wanted no part of that," said Betty, who went to St. Vincent's Hospital in Manhattan at the suggestion of Helen. Betty underwent surgery for torn cartilage at St. Vincent's, and then recuperated at her sister's apartment in New York.

Many weeks later, Betty was visited in New York by a social worker who wanted to know why she hadn't returned to St. Agatha's. "The answer was easy," she said. "I had gotten my first touch of freedom at my sister's in New York, and I wasn't going back."

Betty Doherty did eventually go back to Nanuet, where she found a job caring for patients at the Rockland Psychiatric Center. It was on one of her days off that she met a man of Irish and French-Canadian descent named Kenneth Lavigne. He was a mechanic, who earned a modest living pumping gas and fixing cars at Kip's, a filling station in nearby West Nyack. They soon fell in love and got married, and after three miscarriages Betty finally gave birth to her first child, Roseanne, in 1957.

Betty and Ken tried to have more children after Roseanne, but because of Betty's RH blood factor, her next three pregnancies ended either close to term, at birth, or within a few hours of birth. After the last baby died, the doctors strongly advised Betty not to risk pregnancy again. Despite the emotional pain, which at times overwhelmed Betty, her thoughts always drifted back to her own mother and the comfort she felt in her mother's presence, even if their time together had been so very brief. And because she and Ken didn't want Roseanne growing up without siblings, Betty did something that only in retrospect seemed like a perfectly natural thing to do: She went back to St. Agatha's to inquire about becoming a foster parent.

"Looking back," she said, "St. Agatha's saved my life. I may not have cared for all their rules and regulations and the regimen they put us through, but I don't know whether I would have survived without them."

Needless to say, there were many kids at St. Agatha's who needed loving homes, but the nuns offered the Levignes two young children who had come to St. Agatha's from the New York Foundling Hospital in Manhattan. The children were Dorothy Moore, age four, and her two-year-old brother Billy. Aside from their names and ages, the only thing Betty and Ken knew about their new foster children was that they were biological siblings who had been abandoned by their Irish-Catholic parents.

CHAPTER THREE

The promise of a more idyllic life in the lower-to-middle class suburb of Roosevelt, Long Island, certainly seemed more attractive to Dolores Dunn and her two children, but Robert wasted no time in finding fault with his new surroundings.

The family's first house in Roosevelt, on Park Avenue, was a two-family, red brick structure, with a married couple living upstairs with their two children, and the three Dunns living downstairs. Both families were renters, and the landlord lived nearby.

"Our neighbor upstairs, Mr. Boles, hated me," said Robert. "He couldn't stand my bravado, my self-confidence, and I didn't like him either. He was always going to the landlord, trying to get us evicted."

But even if Mr. Boles hadn't existed, Robert had other complaints. In those days it was almost a source of pride for some families to live in a house that had a big picture window in the living room. The picture window signified affluence, especially to people who grew up in more urban areas, with views mostly of back alleys, fire escapes, and someone else's kitchen.

In Robert Dunn's first house in Roosevelt, the picture window dominated the living room. You could look out and see the world passing by. "But that was the problem," said Robert. "You didn't just look out. You could also look *in*. It was like we were in a fish bowl. Park Avenue was a main thoroughfare for the kids who walked to and from school. And they could easily see us as they walked by. Like they could look into our home and see what was going on. I think I hated that window more than Mr. Boles hated me."

The kitchen sat away from the street, at the other side of the apartment, and on one particular morning, Robert sat there with his mother eating breakfast. It was warm outside, the windows were open, a mother and her son enjoying each other's company in their new house, when suddenly they smelled smoke coming from somewhere in the neighborhood. Robert raced outside, and he could see black smoke billowing from the house on the corner.

"It was a house where a single mother was living with her six children, ages one-six," Robert recalled. "I ran around to the front of their house, and no one was coming outside. Without thinking, I got in through the front door and found all six children huddled together around the baby's bassinette. The mother was nowhere in sight. In fact, she wasn't even home. The children were there alone, and their house was on fire. I picked up the baby and the next youngest child and carried them out the front door."

People from the area had already gathered on the street. Someone had called 911, but the fire department hadn't arrived yet. "I just knew I had to run back inside for the other kids," said Robert. "My mother tried to stop me. Other people shouted, 'Wait for the fire department! Wait for the fire department!' But I was determined. I ran back inside and made my way into the kitchen to check the stove. I don't know how I knew to make sure the gas was turned off, but I checked it and it was off. Then I gathered up the other four children and brought them outside just as the fire trucks were arriving."

The firemen later hailed Robert for risking his life to save six children, but he didn't think it was such a big deal. The fire department even issued him a commendation, and Nassau County Supervisor Thomas Nickerson gave him a medal. His picture made the local papers. "They said I was a hero. I always thought of myself as more of a troublemaker," he said, "but the media attention was nice, and I made sure to smile for the cameras."

Mr. Boles, of course, was convinced that Robert had started the fire. And although Robert knew in his own heart what he had done to save those children, he rarely if ever talked about his heroism again. It was as though the kudos he received for his bravery were unwarranted, and undeserved.

But Robert couldn't have been happier when his mother told him that they would be moving to another house in the neighborhood. The landlord had decided not to renew their lease on Park Avenue, and although everyone in the family suspected the handiwork of Mr. Boles in the landlord's decision, the family happily moved on to a cream-colored, one-family house with a fenced in yard a few blocks away on Grand Street.

Their new neighbors seemed nice enough. Everyone on the block said hello to everyone else. But all was not right inside the Dunns' new home. Dolores Dunn had met a man and married him, a surgeon named Lionel Wardlaw, who had come from Chicago to train at Harlem Hospital. The family grew by one on Grand Street, but the tension was thick inside the house. "Dr. Lionel," as they called him, did not like Dolores' son, Robert, and the feeling was very mutual.

"He was so bizarre," Robert said of his step-father, "that we didn't want other people coming around. By this time, my sister Sharon was already in college, at Stony Brook University, in Long Island, so it was mostly me and Dr. Lionel and my mother. Dr. Lionel had very low self-esteem. Like the rest of us, he suffered a lot of racism growing up in Chicago, and his reaction around us and in public was to use offensive behavior to draw negative attention."

The marriage didn't work out, but not before young Robert punched Dr. Lionel in the face and then had to go to the emergency room so doctors could save his hand, which had been severely wounded on account of the teeth marks left by Dr. Lionel.

The far better memory for Robert Dunn was how he familiarized himself with the many neighborhoods in Roosevelt by getting three different paper routes. His exposure to the racial unrest in his old Queens neighborhood only made him more eager to learn about the racial makeup of his new hometown. Each morning, as he tossed newspapers into neighborhood driveways, he counted the blacks he saw and the whites he saw and who lived where.

"When I started my paper routes," Robert remembered, "I figured that Roosevelt was around sixty-five percent white. But there were 'For Sale' signs on most of the white families' lawns, and by the next year Roosevelt was sixty-five percent black."

The racial makeup of Roosevelt—which included the raising of three eventual home-grown boldface names in Eddie Murphy, Howard Stern, and the great basketball player Dr. J—changed over that quickly. Black people were moving up from the south in droves, and a lot of them were lying about their ages because they'd received an inferior education in the south. There were sixteen-year-old kids in the seventh grade, "big kids," Robert remembered, "and with my mouth I wasn't one to blend in with the scenery. I always had to stand out. I wouldn't take anything from anybody, black or white. I used to tell some of these people, 'Listen, you can kick my ass all you want, but you're still a stupid motherfucker.'

But I needed to keep my black friends close, since whites practically surrounded Roosevelt," he said. "We had to detour around Garden City, Long Island, which was all white, just to get to the mall at Roosevelt Field. And we had to be careful about Merrick, also white turf, right next to Roosevelt Park. Only a bridge separated us and we had to scoot over it quickly because if we were caught over there, we'd get our asses stomped. And vise-versa. If I caught any whites on my turf, they'd get the same treatment."

One of the white boys from Roosevelt High School Robert allegedly beat up was none other than Stern, who later became radio's Number one shock jock. Stern tried for years to get

Robert on his show to talk about the incident, and how Howard had felt victimized by all the black kids in school, but Robert never took the bait.

"I don't remember ever beating up Howard Stern," he said, "but if he says I beat him up, I probably did. In those days you took advantage of people you could beat up, or they took advantage of you. I used to run with another kid named Zany Evans. I know he wound up in jail some years later. Back then, we would grab money from other kids and steal their sneakers. If a kid had a book bag, we'd take that too."

Evans and Dunn also ran this little protection racket in school. "We'd go beat a guy up," Robert said, "and then I'd stop the fight by telling Zany to leave him alone. Then I'd tell the guy we'd just beaten up, 'Say, why don't you give me your lunch money and I'll make sure Zany doesn't bother you for the rest of the school year? Just give it to me every day'"

Sometimes the extortion worked, but even when it didn't, Robert felt empowered by his actions. He was getting back at whites for the bigotry and racist attacks he had endured. He felt superior. It was a feeling he liked.

"Zany Evans was a real tough kid," recalled Charles McIlwain, Roosevelt High's assistant principal when Robert was a student there. "Zany was street-smart, a real hustler. That's what confused me about Robert. He would associate with the toughest kids in school, you know, the kids who were fooling around with drugs and drinking, and fighting, and extortion. But at the same time, he was also with the top kids, the smarter ones, the ones who you knew would succeed. In that way, Robert was impossible to pigeon-hole.

"And Robert never accepted opinions as facts," said the former educator. "He had a legal mind, even at that time in grades nine-twelve. He would go to board meetings and challenge board members about their decisions, whether it had to do with the curriculum, or spending. I found that incredible in a boy his age. He had such a curious mind. He challenged everyone—his classmates, his teachers, even about his grades. If he thought he should have gotten a better grade, he went straight to his teachers and confronted them about his grade. He would eyeball you, and confront you, with no compunction about a challenge.

"It was always a debate, a verbal challenge," said McIlwain. "He was always trying to out-wit you, out-smart. While he was certainly street-smart like Zany—in many ways a hustler like Zany too—but Robert did it with his intelligence. He competed with the top kids in the class. He made the adjustment, no matter which environment he was in. He challenged me too. Sometimes he felt like he didn't want to go to class. He needed a study hall break, he said, or two lunch periods. That's what he was like. You saw him coming. And every time I saw him, I knew, 'That's Robert Dunn,' tall, thin, with an angry look on his face all the time. You knew who he was."

But not even McIlwain was aware initially that during high school Robert also joined a group called the Five Percenters, or the Five Percent Nation, as it was known at the time. The group, an offshoot sect of the Nation of Islam, comprised of young black rebels, many of whom were behind bars. The recruiter who approached Robert explained to him that the name was derived from the belief that blacks had only a five-percent knowledge of self. Though it didn't sound like much, that five percent was supposedly enough to let black people know that they were the original race on earth. Whites, the recruiter said, were created by blacks in a laboratory and developed to the point that they could run the world for a limited period of time. And now that time was up.

He bought into the whole theory. "At the time," he said, "I saw the Nation of Islam as my only salvation. I traveled to the famed Temple No. 7 in Harlem, to hear Minister Louis

Farrakhan, and later to Chicago, to hear sermons delivered by the powerful leader, Elijah Muhammad. Like many other followers of the Nation of Islam, I respected the courage of Dr. Martin Luther King but rejected his nonviolent stance. And I grew even more enraged with white America when, even after King's assassination, blacks continued to be beaten and hosed down in the streets.

I was never a non-violent person," said Robert. "My heroes were Malcolm X, Huey Newton, George Jackson, Stokely Carmichael, and H. Rap Brown—not Martin Luther King or Roy Wilkins, the head of the NAACP. I despised Roy Wilkins especially. I felt he had been co-opted trying to get black people to accept a second-class status. He was such an Uncle Tom, and I wanted to see him hanging from a lamppost. If you were black and you were working with the government, you were a sell-out. That's how I thought."

"My brother didn't hate *all* white people," said his sister Sharon. "He just hated the way society was treating black people. If you became that face, and you were white, he went after you with venom. If on the other hand he saw a white person showing kindness to a black, there is nothing he wouldn't do for that person."

"But I did want to subvert this country," Robert insisted, "because of all it stood for. I started training for the revolution as though I had joined the military. I shot guns and I crawled on my belly, practicing for what I assumed would be the inevitable."

For Robert, the inevitable came on August 21, 1971, when one of his heroes, George Jackson, was gunned down in the San Quentin prison yard.

"I felt like I was going to explode if I didn't do something to attack the pigs for their repression of our people," said Robert. "I was like a self-appointed, righteous commando—I knew I had to strike out and do something. So, as retaliation, I planned to firebomb a small police shack in Roosevelt, Long Island."

The shack he marked for destruction was a wooden structure, about nine feet by twelve feet, with windows on all four sides. He cased the building numerous times and knew that under normal circumstances only one officer would be inside, sitting at a desk with a phone and a police radio. The shack was a perfect target, as it sat on its own little concrete island at the edge of a fork on Nassau Road. And it was white, with a white "pig," as he thought of the officer, sitting inside a white building.

Robert convinced his cousin, Rodney Monteiro, to help him make a Molotov cocktail, a Coca-cola bottle filled with gasoline and stuffed with old rags. At nightfall, the two of them crouched in the bushes on the far side of a narrow alley, about sixty yards from the shack, waiting for the right moment.

I had brought my mother's Playtex gloves," Robert recalled, "as I didn't want to leave fingerprints on the exploded glass. But as I put on the gloves, I realized that, from where we were standing, I might well miss.

'You do it,'" he told Rodney, shoving the home-made device at him. "'You're an excellent baseball player. It's your revolutionary duty to throw this thing because you have the better arm.'"

Rodney refused. "If I throw it, I'm going to have to get a running start," said Rodney. "I'd be exposed, out in the open. You're the brains of the outfit, so you do it."

"No, you throw it," said Robert.

As they argued back and forth, neither of them ever heard the two Nassau County Police officers on foot patrol at the far end of the alley. Training a flashlight on the two conspirators, one of them yelled, "Hey, what the fuck are you guys doing?" In the darkness, Robert took off one of the gloves, pulled the rag out of the Molotov cocktail, dumped out the gasoline, and threw the bottle into the bushes.

"Smells like gasoline back here," said one of the cops, as they closed in.

But the other cop was fixated on the rubber glove Robert was still wearing and the rag he held in his other hand. "You fucking pervert queers," yelled the cop. "Get the hell out of here."

"He must have thought I was jerking off my cousin with my gloved hand," said Robert. "We ran off, lucky to escape. But I had failed to achieve my goal, and this only made me angrier."

CHAPTER FOUR

The very idea of college seemed like a reach to Robert Dunn, and the only way he could actually get accepted somewhere was to go through a summer remedial program. Hofstra University, on Long Island, had one such program called New Opportunities, and Robert applied as a candidate. The program's leader, Frank Smith, was a former member of the Nation of Islam, and he saw a lot of himself in the younger Dunn.

"The program was for students who didn't have the requisite average for getting in, or requisite SAT scores," said Smith. "It was really an affirmative action program to take poor students from the community and give them increased financial aid and increased support services to help them navigate their way through the university."

Robert, of course, made an immediate impression on Smith. "He was a brilliant young man, but also kind of crazy," said Smith. "Another man who knew Robert well was Canute Parris, a black professor and the chairman of the African Studies Department. He knew Robert through his work in the community, and he told me about this outstanding young man who was a little bit disorganized and unsure of himself. But he said Robert was brilliant, and that I had to accept him into the program. I could tell immediately that Robert was brilliant, but he needed a lot of direction, a lot of mentoring and support. He was radical and unusual."

"Frank Smith ran the program like an educational boot camp," said Robert, "and I found myself surrounded by tutors who insisted on mandatory study hours and by counselors who tried to break me down and make me less violent. I did everything I could to get kicked out of the program, but Frank never gave up on me."

"He's right. It was like a boot camp," Smith conceded. "That's what those students needed. They lacked discipline. They lacked focus. Because we didn't judge these potential students based on their average and SAT scores, we had to use different criteria. We had three interviews with them—one individual interview, and two group interviews. We judged their motivation and their level of potential; whether or not there was a strong support person in their family, whether or not they ever succeeded at anything in life. We probably had five hundred candidates for maybe fifteen slots. It was very competitive to get in. But I knew from the start that Robert would get in because of Canute, who was my mentor. Canute said I simply had to accept him. Robert didn't know he was going to get accepted, but I did.

"I was with Robert every day that summer," said Smith, "and we disciplined him, along with all the other candidates. He didn't get off easy just because of my relationship with Canute. We showed him how to organize himself, how to discipline his mind, his body, and we developed the potential that was inherent in him. The key for all the candidates was that they had to have the potential. Otherwise, there would be nothing to develop. And Robert had big potential."

"With Frank's help," Robert said, "I completed the program and was able to start at Hofstra as a freshman."

Thinking he knew everything there was to know about his black heritage from his experiences with the Five Percenters and the Nation of Islam, Robert signed up for an African Studies course. The first time Robert attempted to share his knowledge in class, his professor for this particular course, Dr. Calistus Ndlobu, from Zimbabwe, shut him down immediately. Calling Robert out in front of the class, Professor Ndlobu said he couldn't fathom how a person with this belief system could even get into college.

"He ordered me to read forty books on African history and keep my mouth shut in class until I'd finished them," said Robert. "When I read the books, I realized how ignorant I'd been for so long, and I was truly ashamed of it."

And like always, he turned that embarrassment and shame inward. Nevertheless, with the help of people like Frank Smith, Canute Parris and Professor Ndlobu, Robert worked hard in college, established a few real friendships, even with white students, and began to feel like a whole person. "Education saved me," he said. "I learned that I could have a rich and all-inclusive life, and even give back to others."

"During his Hofstra years, Robert always came back to Roosevelt High School to visit with me," said Charles McIlwain. "I would ask him questions about college, you know, like, 'How are you doing, Robert?'

"He'd say, 'Fine.'

"Is it difficult?"

"He'd say, 'No.' But then he'd always add, 'I'm going to be a lawyer one of these days, and I'm going to change the world. I have the answers to all the social, academic and political problems.' He just had that air about him," said McIlwain.

"Robert never gave up his radicalism, and in my view that was a good thing," said Smith. "But in the process he became more of a thinker and more of a political analyst. During that first summer, I invited someone from the Hofstra Board of Trustees to speak to the students. She was a pediatrician, and I remember vividly how Robert cursed her out. I said, 'Man, you can't speak to her like that.' But that was Robert. But as he grew at Hofstra and matured in his political analysis, that kind of thing left him. And it was replaced by some humanity and a great sophistication of thought.

"I knew early on that Robert would probably become a lawyer," said Smith. "I could see his career, probably before he did. I knew he had the gift of verbosity, the gift of analysis. I knew he could take words and twist them any kind of way to have you thinking you were going north when you were really going south."

Robert eventually applied to the University of Southern California Law School, and was accepted. He graduated in 1980, passed the Bar exam in both New York and California, and began practicing law.

"I was drawn to law because I saw it as my revolutionary duty," he said. "I learned everything I could so I could defend the rights of my people, while at the same time undermine the existing political structure because that structure was predicated on the exploitation of my people. The racism I experienced in my childhood and the anger I carried as a result had propelled me to attend college. It wasn't so I could one day get a good job and make a lot of money. I went to college and then law school to better learn how to attack the society. I felt my people were being abused on a daily basis, that we were the downtrodden ones, and it was my responsibility to do something about it."

After Robert got his law degree, a woman he knew from high school in Roosevelt, Syretta McKnight, who had just won a seat on the local board of education, recommended him to become the school board lawyer, and he got the job.

"So now I was seeing him every two weeks at board meetings," said McIlwain. "By now he had calmed down somewhat. He had a real sense of direction and purpose. He was out there, as he said, for the people. He said it wasn't about money for him. It was about finding answers to poverty, to all the anger in the community, to the dropout rate at the high school, to black-on-black crime, to race relations. He had a broader scope as to what he wanted, which was to be involved in all these issues.

"And while he was always a good, loving person, it always came back to his anger," said McIlwain. "He stood up at a board meeting once in front of me and two other black board members, Joe Farmer and Phil Smith. My responsibility was grades seven-eight. Phil Smith's was nine-ten. And Joe Farmer's was eleven-twelve. Joe Farmer was also the administrator in charge.

Robert would go to a board meeting and challenge Joe Farmer by calling him 'Farmer Joe.' And then he would call Phil Smith 'Bigot Smith.' Mind you, this was at a board meeting. Robert wanted them fired because they didn't have a good solid black history program at the high school. Robert kept himself in the limelight by making those kinds of statements. He and I would talk about it, and he would just laugh. He liked to put people on the spot like that."

But Robert also knew he needed to tone down his style slightly, and doing something about it meant becoming, in his words, "a straight-laced square.

"My hustle," he said, "which had served me well on the streets, had to be refined in the courtroom, and augmented with hard work, painful research, and an understanding of what it was like to be responsible for someone else's life. For the first time in my life, I felt like I had something to lose."

"By that point," McIlwain said, "I could see that Robert was beginning to shine. Other people saw it too. I will never forget Dan Abrams of MSNBC saying to me that Robert was going to be the next Johnny Cochran."

CHAPTER FIVE

In the understandably biased words of her new foster mother, "Dorothy was the most beautiful, adorable little girl.

"She reminded me of the Ivory Snow baby," Betty Levigne recalled. "Dorothy and Roseanne would sit watching TV— these little girls, each with a ponytail, and the dog would come up behind them and grab their ponytails. And Dot would laugh and laugh. She began her life with us as a normal, happy girl."

At least that's what Betty thought. But Dorothy's problems began with her initial confusion about her roots. "At certain points in our lives," said Roseanne, "Dorothy would say to Billy, 'Are we Levigne? Or Moore?' She always knew that she and Billy were blood relations, and I wasn't. Those things were definitely said throughout our childhood. Billy might be playing with me, and Dorothy would get upset that he wasn't playing with her."

But once the territorial issues were settled the three children always wound up playing together in the yard. Dorothy and Roseanne were Bluebirds together at the local Baptist church, and according to Betty, the three children behaved like most siblings in most families.

"But Dot always knew that I was the 'country mommy,'" said Betty. "I never tried to take the place of her real mother and father. I said to her, 'If anybody asks you, just tell them you were my engagement gift, and leave it at that. Nobody has to know your business.' At one time we did ask Dot and Billy whether they wanted to have their names changed to Levigne, and they said no."

Betty believed Dorothy wanted to hold on to her birth name because it represented at least one thing from her past that she could call her own. "She clearly knew she had been rejected by her own family," said Betty, "so that had to be painful. When she was very young, I had to call a psychiatrist because she tried to jump out of a second-floor window after a visit with one of her biological parents. I was concerned about that. The therapist spoke with Dorothy, but did not tell me anything. In those days, they didn't say much about health issues or family issues. As foster parents, we were just responsible to bring them up in our home. I questioned the people at St. Agatha's about whether they knew any history of disease in the Moore family, but they said they would only tell us if it became necessary." It never did.

"She came into our home as a little girl and saw what it was like to be raised by a mother who cared," said Roseanne. "We will probably never know why her natural parents left her and her brother to live in an orphanage, and while Dorothy must have come to St. Agatha's with some emotional scars from infancy, at least she had the chance to live in a loving home."

Dorothy rarely expressed her feelings, no matter how she felt. "She never once talked about her biological parents," said Betty. "I believe she had two older biological siblings, but she had no connection to them whatsoever."

The relationships inside the Levigne home started to fray somewhat as cliques began to form under a new social order in high school. Although they shared a room well into their high school years, due largely to the fact that the house was so small, Dorothy and Roseanne each wound up hanging out with different circles of friends. The blond, cherub-faced Roseanne was a high school cheerleader who spent hours each day practicing with her cheerleader friends and worrying about weekend football games. Dorothy, whose dark hair matched her dark eyes, ran with a much rougher crowd.

Dorothy had difficulty in school from the beginning, and by high school she was clearly a "Special-Ed" student who couldn't get by without a lot of help. It didn't help that she was also a "partier," according to Rosanne, who tried to encourage her to go out for sports. "She was very athletic," said Roseanne. "She could hit a baseball further than any of us. She was a fast runner. She was always physically skilled."

So skilled, in fact, that Dorothy would talk about one day becoming a gym teacher. "In gym, she could climb the ropes to the top. She could do everything," said Betty. "But as soon as she got mixed up with a fast crowd, she became much harder to handle."

"Dorothy always gravitated to the kids at St. Agatha's," said Roseanne. "Even though they had no idea that she too came from St. Agatha's, they accepted her for who she was. There was this time when a friend of mine was not getting along with a friend of Dorothy's, and there was going to be this big fight. And I remember saying, 'Look, we need to cut this out. This is ridiculous.' And here I'm talking to this big black girl who could've squashed me like a bug, but she didn't because I was Dorothy's sister. Dorothy often got me into trouble, but she always got me out of trouble."

The big black girl Roseanne remembered was one of Dorothy's closest friends in town. According to Roseanne, Dorothy always felt more comfortable around blacks and Hispanics.

Dorothy dropped out of high school in her senior year, and ran away from home with Alfonso Garcia, a young Hispanic boy she knew from St. Agatha's.

"We first met when we lived across the street from each other in Nanuet," said Garcia. "She was friends with the daughters of the people who took me in. I also started out at St. Agatha's, and went to live with the Stewart family, across the street from the Levignes, when I was twelve years old. Dorothy would come across the street to see Cheryl and Monica, who were sisters. They used to hang out and go everywhere together. We were just friends in the beginning."

Alfonso and Dorothy got much closer when they started working together in the laundry room Rockland State Hospital, a psychiatric facility in nearby Orangeburg, NY. "We handled the laundry for the entire psychiatric center," said Garcia. "She was a nice person, a hard worker, and she got along with everybody. She was kind-hearted, with brown hair, always petite and skinny. No enemies. If someone needed money, she'd give it to them, even though she had so little money herself. If you asked her for something, and she had it, she gave it to you."

They always car-pooled to work, said Garcia. "Once in a while she would get another ride. She didn't drive, didn't have a license. She always needed to get a ride."

On one particular warm night the two camped out together in Dorothy's back yard, "and that's when it happened.

"I never knew if I was her first," said Garcia. "She didn't say and I didn't ask."

Dorothy vanished from Nanuet soon after she found out that she had become pregnant. "She was never the same after she became involved with Alfonso," said Betty. "There was no talking to her because she got involved with drugs."

When Dorothy did return to her foster mother's home, she was one month away from giving birth.

"She showed up with a dog and a bird and a belly out to here," said Betty. "I said, 'You can come in, but no bird. And since I already have a dog, no dog either.' I asked no further questions about with whom she had been or where she had been. I was just happy to have her back. I got her to a clinic. I got her to start seeing a doctor regularly so her pregnancy could be monitored. Then we prepared the house for a baby. We got a changing table. My husband put the crib together for her. But neither of us asked questions. We just went forward with the next thing that had to be done."

Betty and the family nurtured Dorothy through the birth of her first child, a baby boy, William Moore, whom everyone called Willie.

"After Willie was born she would take him out with her until all hours of the night," said Betty. "He was an infant! Finally, my husband said to her, 'Look, you can go out whenever you want, and come home whenever you want, but you can't be out with a baby until the middle of the night. That's just plain wrong.' So we got her a babysitter that only cost her five cents an hour, which was all she could afford because she had no job and no money. But by paying even the nickel it made her feel more responsible."

Betty looked on with amusement as Dorothy adjusted to the stress of being a first-time mother. "She had Willie on a bottle with strained food coming out of the bottle. I remember the first time I saw this," said Betty. "Willie was about a year old. He was in a hi-chair sucking strained food out of a bottle. I looked at her and said, 'Not here, honey. Want to see something?' So I took some mashed potatoes and put it in a bowl, put a little gravy on it, and he had a ball. He made a mess, but he had a good time. I said, 'That's what he needs, Dot. Table food.'

"She said, 'Well, he doesn't always eat it, Ma.'

"I said, 'Well, you have to encourage him. Cut it up small and give it to him. Believe me, he'll eat it.'"

The care Betty provided to Dorothy and her son Willie would only last for a short time. "Then one day I came home from work and she had her bags packed and said she was taking the baby to live with a friend," said Betty. "The next time I saw her, which was a few years later, she came home with a second son, Allan, who was already a toddler. And she was even pregnant again with a third child.

"She said there had been a fire in the summer colony in Spring Valley, where she was living, and so she came home to us again," said Betty. "When my husband came home that night, he said, 'Whoa, what is this, another sleepover?' Because of the fire, she had no heat and no electricity, and that's why she came home. And just like always, we took her in. She always came back to this loving home. I never once questioned her as to where she had been or who she was with. I never said, 'How could you do this or that?' I was just happy to have her home, even if it was only to give her a meal and let her take a shower. She came home because she knew there was love here."

CHAPTER SIX

In 1989, Robert married Rebecca Monseratte, whom everyone called Kitty. A gorgeous 5'6" Puerto Rican with very long black hair, Kitty worked for a Harlem-based nonprofit organization that placed children in foster homes. Robert had never known anyone like her, and the two fell madly in love. And when Robert loved, it was passionately, intense and all-consuming. For a while, everything went extremely well for Robert and Kitty. They were a couple with two incomes. They saved money, planned for the future, and had plenty of unprotected sex. They both said they wanted children, but for some reason she wasn't getting pregnant. The way Robert remembered it, Kitty didn't really want to become pregnant, and to him this was causing great problems in the relationship. He wanted her to go to a fertility expert. She refused. And he took her refusal as a sign that she really didn't love him.

"That's how dumb I was," he said. "If only I had stopped long enough to allow myself to experience real intimacy, I would have realized that she was afraid of the entire childbearing process and needed to be brought along slowly."

Kitty, of course, saw it differently. "I felt the same way about children as him," she said. "I wanted to have children too. But it was not easy for me to become pregnant. I had fibroids and endometriosis, which caused me extreme pains in my uterus. Pregnancy just never happened. There was a time in our relationship when we felt we were ready to have a baby, and then things just changed. We were having problems in our marriage, and I felt that bringing a child into that environment might not be the right thing to do. I don't think a child would have resolved the situation between us."

Nevertheless, Kitty suggested adoption. Robert was only lukewarm to the idea, and he only agreed to it on the condition they have their own child first. "I thought it was my responsibility to procreate," he said.

"Sure, I would have adopted," she said. "I could have gone either way. But Robert is a handful, to begin with. He needs all the attention to be on him. He could become jealous of the cat. He needed to feel secure. He needed to be stroked. He needed to know that he was loved unconditionally, twenty-four/seven, and that was a handful."

Robert started looking at his life as a waste without a child. He couldn't forgive himself. "When I was younger," he said, "all I wanted was an older brother. Then, when I got a little older, all I wanted was a younger brother. I kept begging my mother for a brother, and I remember the day when my mother told me, 'Look, Bobby, that ship has sailed. I'm not having any more children. You're just going to have to learn to live with that fact. It ain't happening.'"

"I remember saying to my mother, out of anger, 'Okay, I'm just going to have my own child, a son. And when I do have a son, I'm going to have the relationship with him that I didn't have with my father, and couldn't have with my brother because you didn't give me a brother.'"

It was then that his mother told him that she had lost a baby through miscarriage before him, and lost another baby through miscarriage after him. "And that surely didn't get through my thick scull," he said. "I mean, if I couldn't feel compassion for Kitty when I was thirty-five, I must have been completely hopeless at eleven."

Kitty didn't just blame Robert for the utter lack of communication in their marriage. She also took on a lot of the blame herself. "It was both of us," she said. "I think we were both ready to be married. But I don't think we were ready to deal with everything that comes with marriage."

For one thing, they kept totally different hours. She is a morning person. He was more himself at night. "By the time I left in the morning to go to work, he was just crawling into bed to go to sleep," she said. "By the time I got home to hang out and settle in, his day was continuing into its next phase. He worked constantly, and by the time he got home at, say, 11 pm, he would want me to sit with him while he ate dinner, and I was ready for sleep. Between watching TV, being on the phone, going through his work at home, smoking marijuana, he could be up all night. So we had totally different hours, and I didn't smoke marijuana. It bothered me that he did. But it made him relax and it made him eat. With his Crohn's disease, relaxing and eating were important things for him, so smoking made it easier for him to relax and eat. Smoking helped him in that regard, so that was okay. But bringing a child into the world at that time would have exacerbated all our problems."

Kitty knew the marriage wasn't working and that a breakup would only be a matter of time. "Several things led up to that breakup," she said. "We were both at fault. I'm not blaming him, because I had a lot to do with it too. He was extremely needy, and I'm the opposite. I'm very quiet, reserved. I will absolutely show you love. He would say that I had a lot of cat characteristics. I'd show him love, stroke up on him, hug him and kiss him, and he'd say, 'Okay, that's enough.' I would want some attention too, and he would give me a little, and then say, 'That's enough.' And that was okay with me because I was not that needy. And then there would times he would just flip out and lose his mind, scream, curse and carry on.

"As an example," she said, "we would go food shopping. He'd want a can of creamed corn. I wanted regular corn. He would take the can of creamed corn, dump it in the shopping cart, and I would take a regular can of corn, saying that was what I wanted. And he'd say, 'Put it back. I want the creamed corn.'

"And then I'd say, 'Fine, you have your creamed corn, and I will have my regular corn.' And he would say no," she said. "It had nothing to do with money. After all, how much is a can of corn, seriously? So he took my can of regular corn and put it back on the shelf. I looked at him, and I could be stubborn too, so I took the can back off the shelf, and put it back in the shopping cart. I said, 'You can have your creamed corn, but I am going to have my regular corn.'"

That was not what Robert wanted to hear. "He grabbed my can," Kitty said, "and he looked at me, and he said, 'If you try to put this can of corn back into the shopping cart, you are not going to believe what will happen.' So he put it back on the shelf, and I took it again and put it back into the shopping cart. He then took the can off the shelf and he threw it down the aisle and started screaming like a madman. He went absolutely ballistic, screaming, 'You're stubborn. You don't listen. We only need one can.' I looked straight ahead, acting like I didn't know him. And then I walked out of the supermarket. He kept yelling, "I know you can hear me.' Of course, I could hear him. Everyone in the supermarket heard him. Over a can of corn."

But the issues between them ran much deeper than a disagreement over a can of corn. Neither was trying to dictate what the other ate at home. They were just two extremely strong-willed people with chosen battlegrounds that often took a jealous turn. "I would get dressed for work in the morning," Kitty said, "and if he didn't like what I was wearing, he would want me to take it off and start over. And if I didn't take it off, he would wait for me to take off my clothes later so he could pick them up and throw them away. Crazy stuff. I wasn't used to that kind of behavior, and it was certainly not good for a long-term relationship.

"At a certain point," she said, "I had had enough. I had more than enough. Especially when he would say things like, 'This is my apartment.' I could never feel entirely comfortable being in an apartment, and being married, when my husband is constantly reminding me that we are in *his* apartment. I don't know anyone who would feel comfortable around that.

"I'd come home, looking for a certain pair of shoes, or a certain pair of boots," she said, "and they would sometimes be gone because I wore them and I must have looked too sexy in them when he wasn't with me. I finally told him, 'I can't do this anymore.'

"We tried therapy," she said, "but I think he went just to humor me. And then he just didn't go anymore."

"Kitty and I broke up just seven months after our wedding," said Robert. "Looking back, it was one of the worst decisions I ever made in my life."

CHAPTER SEVEN

Dorothy Moore's third child was a daughter whom she
named Elizabeth, which was her foster mother's real first name.
"After Elizabeth was born," said Betty, "Dorothy told me what
she had planned to do, which was put the baby up for adoption.
I said, 'It's your decision. If you feel like it's the best thing to
do, then do it. You just might be giving the child a better start
in life.'

"Then, almost a year after Elizabeth was adopted," Betty
continued, "Dorothy said to me, 'You know, I've thought about
it, and I think I'd like to take Elizabeth back.'

"And I said, 'Sit down a minute, I want to talk to you.' I
said, 'Listen, this has nothing to do with you. This has nothing
to do with me. It has to do with this child. You cannot play
ping pong with a baby. You can't go back and forth. You have
to make a final decision, and stick to it. If you want to try to
get the baby back, you have to go to the judge. You would have
to prove you could take care of the child. In order to rescind
the adoption, you will have to convince the court that you are
capable, that the adoption was a mistake, and this other family
would have to agree, which in all likelihood they won't. You'd
be breaking the hearts of these people, taking their child away.
Legally she is their child now, not yours.'"

Dorothy never tried to get the child back. Instead, she went
on to have two more sons with the same man who fathered her
second child, Allan.

"She did try her best to care for those three young boys,"
said Betty, "but each of them had problems."

The boys' older half-brother Willie Moore believes those
problems began and ended with the Irish-Catholic man who
eventually replaced his father as his mother's lover. For one
thing, this new boyfriend already had a wife and a couple of
children, and even though Willie was probably too young to
understand the complexities surrounding the double life this

man was leading, he could plainly see that the new man in his mother's bed was also a drunk who abused her on several occasions, both verbally and physically.

Willie's father Alfonso Garcia pressed Dorothy to send their son down to Florida, where he was living. She knew her little boy would be safer with his father, and so she obliged. She certainly had enough on her hands caring for Allan and his two younger brothers, John and Jesse. But Willie only stayed with his father for a short time, and soon he traveled back to upstate New York, back to where his mother and brothers were living, back into, as he described it, "a living hell.

"When he got mad," Willie said of his mother's boyfriend, "he would take an axe to the house and tear up the walls. He was a very, very heavy drinker. He drank every single day. I remember one day, I was probably four or five, and I was crying because I wanted candy. He was drunk and when he heard me screaming, he grabbed my head and tried to crack it on the toilet seat. When my father and his brother found out what he had done to me, they told him in no uncertain terms that if he ever touched me again, drunk or sober, they would come back and kill him.

"Jail was his second home," said Willie. "This man was 6-3 and 250 pounds of pure muscle, and my mother was 5-2 and 90 pounds soaking wet, and he would throw her around like a rag doll. She called me up one day and told me that he was holding her and my three little brothers hostage in this log cabin where they all lived in Monticello, New York. My brother Johnny had been crying because he didn't want to take a bath, and his father reacted by holding Johnny's head under the water, trying to drown him. When my mother tried to intervene, he loaded up his father's shotgun, and he said to her, 'If you call the cops, I'll blow you away. Then I'll kill the cops, and then I'll kill myself.'"

The constant abuse Dorothy suffered eventually resulted in her packing up her younger three sons, along with Willie, and taking them all down to Willie's father in Florida.

"Even though we had broken up years before," said Garcia, "we always remained good friends. Unfortunately, though, she only stayed with me in Florida for a few months. Then she found another place to stay, not far from my house. Then she started souring on Florida entirely. I told her she was being impatient, that she needed to give it more time in Florida, but she didn't listen. She had tried to find work in Laundromats. She tried to get jobs cleaning hotel rooms, but nothing was happening. Prospective employers said to her, 'Don't call us. We'll call you.' She became annoyed over everything, and so she took her three young sons and left. There was never any question about Willie, who was now fourteen. He was staying with me."

Florida was the last place Garcia ever saw Dorothy. But he did talk to her often on the phone. Those conversations were mostly about Willie: Was he being good? How was he doing in school? "We would talk about the possibility of her other kids coming back down so they could spend time with Willie, but it never happened. I knew the other boys. They were good kids, but they were kids. Sometimes they had to be disciplined. But it was never anything bad. I used to work for a vending company, and when they were with me they would wait for me every night to see what kind of goodies I brought back for them. For the brief time she had a place of her own in Florida, I helped her out with candy, chips, sandwiches, all from the vending machines. Instead of throwing it away, I always brought things to the neighborhood kids. Most of it went to Dorothy, just to help her to try and make it. I remembered what it was like when I first came down to Florida, the struggle. So I knew how it was for her.

"We continued talking on the phone for a long time after she went back to New York," he said. "I knew her boyfriend from way back. Down deep he was an all-right guy. But she could have done better, in my opinion."

○

CHAPTER EIGHT

Oliver Smith would sneak into the courtroom just so he could sit down in the back and watch Robert Dunn work. But Smith was hardly some wide-eyed youngster who got hooked on trials by watching all the lawyer shows on TV. He was an accomplished lawyer in his own right, a Caribbean native with a law degree from Jamaica who came to New York in 1986, passed the New York State Bar Exam, and got a job working for a downtown law firm that had been leasing office space to Robert.

"When I first met him, he was a little leery of who I was," said Smith. "I had come from Jamaica, and a lot of people in New York seemed suspicious of me, I think mostly because I was Caribbean and I hadn't gone to an American Bar Association-approved law school. I definitely needed assistance in finding my way around the New York courts, and I would ask Robert questions, and suddenly he was showing me around the courts, especially the criminal courts.

"I did watch a lot of his trials," said Smith. "He was the best lawyer I have ever seen, bar none. And I'm not just saying that because of the personal relationship I developed with him. I started practicing in Jamaica in '84, and I've seen lawyers in the Caribbean, and I've seen years of lawyers in America, and as a trial lawyer no one was ever better than Robert Dunn."

What made Robert so good, Smith said, was his preparation, the way he dove into his cases. "He would spend countless hours dissecting the case, surgically breaking it down," he said. "He would decide on his theme for the case and how he would portray it. He prepared his cross-examinations meticulously, and was very thorough in preparing his clients for testimony. His courtroom effectiveness came from that preparation."

Other lawyers, to be sure, routinely spend many, many hours and days preparing for courtroom battle, but what set Robert apart, according to Smith, was his delivery. "Practicing and preparing is one thing," said Smith, "but showing up for the big game and delivering is something else. Robert was very charismatic. He had juries eating out of his hands. He could read people. He knew how to speak to jurors. He would never speak above them, and he communicated with them very effectively.

"Two aspects of his courtroom skills that set him apart were his cross-examination and his closings," said Smith. "He was the best cross-examiner I have ever seen, and anybody who has ever seen him cross-examine a witness, from judges to prosecutors on the other side and colleagues who have sat in on his trials, will all say the same thing. He was the best cross-examiner, bar none. A lot of things that I now use in my cross-examinations I actually stole from watching him. His philosophy of cross-examining, which I have adopted, had a style which he called 'closing the doors.' He would close all the doors so that when he asked the question that he needed to ask, he got the answer he wanted. There would be no other answers because the doors would have all been closed. A lot of lawyers will ask the important question too early in the game, and they wind up giving the witness a way out. When Robert cross-examined, there was no way out.

"I remember his cross-examination of an undercover officer," Smith continued. "And he got the undercover officer to admit that he used cocaine, that he sampled cocaine to legitimize his undercover status as a street dealer. Attorneys understand that undercover officers must do certain things to advance their credibility. But as a rule, you never can get them to admit that they actually used the drugs they were supposedly selling. But Robert was able to cross-examine the guy so effectively in the end the guy had to give it up. And when Robert was finished cross-examining him, the guy was so battered that he couldn't find his way out of the courtroom. He got up. He started walking towards the judge. They said, 'Not this way, sir.' Then he headed in the direction of the door to the jury room. The poor cop actually had to be led out of the courtroom."

In 1991, Robert became a regular commentator for Court TV, and in 1994, he became a frequent TV contributor to the O.J. Simpson story. Robert's law practice was thriving, and people on the street were recognizing him from TV. He was hardly what one would consider a star, but he had become enough of a big shot to at least impress his barber.

The Superstar Barber Shop Robert frequented on West 124th Street in Harlem was right out of an Eddie Murphy movie. It was the kind of hangout where black men of all ages would gather to argue politics, gossip about celebrities, and one-up each other with an unending stream of dirty jokes. And because he was on television, Robert was one of the barbershop's best-known characters.

"It's a place where the brothers can go and bond with one another and understand what each one of us is going through at certain times in our lives," said Robert's long-time barber Dennis Mitchell. "The barber shop is a refuge, a place where you can get away from a lot of things, a place where you don't have to be anything other than yourself, a place where boys can do what boys do, but without any of us judging anyone else."

In Mitchell's eyes, Robert occupied a unique place in the pantheon of his customers. "Rob was one of the only customers who ever came in wearing a suit," Mitchell said. "Don't get me wrong, there were other customers who wore suits and ties, but not like Rob. He was so down to earth. Nothing we did or said shocked him. He was us. He could engage in the things we talked about. A lot of the men who came in wearing suits worked downtown. You'd get the sense that they wanted to be 'above' what we talked about, aloof from the conversations, and not be a part of it, as in, 'I'm not a part of this no matter what color I am.' But Rob wasn't like that. When we were downtown, Rob held it downtown. But when we were uptown and Rob came in, even though he was dressed for downtown, you'd never know he was a downtown guy, you'd never know he was that fine lawyer. Nothing said in that barber shop ever surprised him, and nothing he ever said surprised us. He fell right in. He was like a chameleon. When he was downtown, he acted accordingly. But when he came uptown, he was just like the rest of us."

The two men soon developed a relationship outside the barber shop. "We went out to dinner a lot," Mitchell said. "He was my confidante. Even though I was not his client, everything we talked about was remained in the area of 'lawyer-client privilege.' Everything was off the record. I talked about my family, my wife, or about a particular problem, and he would give me legal advice, friendly advice, whatever the situation called for. I'd go to him sometimes with tears in my eyes, or I'd be mad at someone for something, and naturally I'd want him to represent me. And he'd talk me off the ledge, so to speak. If I was complaining about my wife, it was Rob who would remind me that we were a great couple, that we were beautiful together, and he would always advise me to work it out."

Mitchell described their friendship as "two peas in a pod."

"He would tell his lies, I would tell my lies," said Mitchell. "And we'd complement each other's lies.

"I got stopped once for a seatbelt infraction, but when my name went through the system they found an old warrant against me," Mitchell said. "So they took me to jail, and I'm frantically trying to get Rob to come down for me. And the cops said, 'Relax, you'll get out tomorrow.'

"I said, 'I need my boy to come down and get me out now.' Well, Rob came and pushed me right through the process and got me out. He did what he had to do. He even brought me a sandwich.

"I would advise him too," said Mitchell. "He would talk to me about his relationships, and he would talk to me about his health. He was not good about taking care of his health."

The barber, in fact, was with Robert Dunn on the day in 1995 that his real health nightmare began. Robert came into The Superstar Barber Shop that day and waited for Mitchell to finish with another customer.

"Rob sat for a while waiting, and then he got into the chair," said Mitchell. "I was cutting his hair when he suddenly went into a cold sweat. I asked him, 'Are you all right, man? You just started sweating out of nowhere.'

"He said, 'I don't know what's going on with me. But lately it's been happening to me,'" recalled Mitchell. "He had Crohn's disease. He said, 'Give me a minute. I'm going to the bathroom.' He got out of the chair, went into the bathroom, and I heard him collapse. I ran in and helped him up. He was conscious. I walked him back to the chair and sat him back down. And of course he tried to make it look like it wasn't that serious. I called for an ambulance. He said he didn't want to go. I said, 'Well, too bad. You don't have a choice.'"

Robert's heartbeat was erratic and his blood pressure was low, but he seemed to be all right by the time EMS reached Mt. Sinai Medical Center, across town on Fifth Ave. "So there he was laying in the ER, and he called me over and told me to bend down so he could whisper something to me," said Mitchell. "I got closer to him and I didn't know what to expect. Maybe he wanted to go through some confessional. So I put my ear close to his mouth, and he said, 'Reach into my sock, and get that joint out of my sock.'"

No hospital bed was available that night, so Robert had to spend most of the evening in the ER. "I told the staff I was a busy man," Robert recalled. "I told them I had a real estate closing in the morning, and that I must be available to my clients. Against the doctors' advice, I left."

Robert returned to the barber shop about a month later. He got his hair washed, cut, and then suddenly he was back in the shop's bathroom again, where he promptly passed out again. "He was more coherent this time," Mitchell recalled, "so I made a joke. I said, 'Damn, Rob, if you don't want to pay for the haircut, you don't have to act like you're falling out all the time.'"

The EMS arrived on the scene again, but this time they took him to NYU Medical Center, where he underwent a battery of tests.

His mother Dolores and his sister Sharon were there when a doctor came in. The good news, the doctor said, was that Robert's liver was good, his kidneys were functioning properly, and his arteries were cleaner than he had ever seen in an African-American male of similar age. Robert figured that was a result of his Nation of Islam days, when he gave up eating pork.

And the bad news? "He said that I had a severely enlarged heart," Robert said, "and if I were to live any longer, I would need a heart transplant. I said, 'Get this motherfucker out of here before I knock him out.'"

"You don't understand," the doctor said. "It's just your heart. Everything else is great. Once you get another heart, you'll be fine."

Robert thought the guy was out of his mind, that they'd give him another heart and four months later he'd be dead.

He told the doctor to forget it, and proceeded to keep his condition a secret from everyone but his mother and sister, a few cousins, and a law partner. He didn't even tell his new girlfriend, but she began to sense his illness during their lovemaking.

"My breathing was labored," he recalled. "I had difficulty keeping an erection, and I even faked a couple of orgasms. Eventually she confronted me, and I told her part of the truth - that I'd been diagnosed with a heart condition. I didn't tell her I needed a heart transplant. The last thing I wanted to feel around her was my own vulnerability."

Eventually, he placed himself under the care of a top heart

transplant specialist at Columbia-Presbyterian Hospital, the leading transplant facility in New York.

"We're not just here to give you a transplant," the doctor said. "We're here to help you keep your own heart for as long as possible. Then, if a transplant becomes necessary, we'll ship you over to the transplant unit." A transplant didn't appear imminent. Robert was relieved.

CHAPTER NINE

In the fall of 1997, Robert suffered a stroke. His speech was slurred and he could hardly walk. He made an appointment with a Chinese herbalist, who took his pulse and said, "Too far gone. You need Western medicine. You need another heart."

By April 1998, he was back at Columbia-Presbyterian. "Your readings are inconsistent with life," a doctor told him. "Your cardiac output is 0.08 and 2.2 is usually considered a crisis stage. You need a mechanical heart and you need it today."

Robert lost it. "I went ballistic," he said. "I was screaming, 'A mechanical heart instead of a transplant? You mean it's not bad enough that my chest has to be cracked open so I could get somebody else's heart? Now you're telling me that my chest has to be cracked open so they could put some machine inside of me before I even get to the point where they have to open me up again for the real transplant? Well, fuck that.' I still wasn't accepting that my own heart wouldn't recover."

The doctor said, "Look, you're dying."

Robert said, "I am not dying. Even with two IV poles in me I'll prove I'm not dying. I'll run around this entire hospital five times." And he did start running around the cardiac floor, poles and all. "It was like outrage and denial were keeping me alive," he said.

But the doctor was having none of it. "Oh, no," he said. "You'll definitely need a transplant. And a mechanical heart is a bridge to that transplant."

Robert told him, "If I have to be the first person to live without a heartbeat, I will be that person, because I'm not dying and I'm not getting a mechanical heart."

"I remember how Robert cursed out the doctor," said Oliver Smith. "And he did jog around the hospital just to show how fit he was. Robert always wore his emotions on his sleeve. If he's upset with you, you're going to know it. And if you are as close to him, as I am, he could curse me out one minute and hug me the next. Hearing he needed a new heart was very difficult for him to handle. He went through a contemplative and self-examining process. He was very much against a heart transplant."

It didn't help that his barber, Dennis Mitchell, also had difficulty accepting that his friend needed another heart. "I was worried, though," he said. "I would see him in the hospital. I shaved him there, gave him haircuts there, and when he'd talk about what the doctors had wanted for him, I would agree with him. I remember saying, 'You're only forty-two years old, man.'

"And he said, 'I know, I know. These people don't know who they're dealing with. I don't need anyone else's heart.'

"Then he said something to me in the hospital that I can never forget," said Mitchell. "He said, 'Man if I can only live six more years. Six more fucking years, and I'll be all right.'

"I said, 'Why six years? Why that number?'

"He said, 'I don't know. I'm just talking. I just made up six years. I don't know why.'

"They talked about putting valves in him from a pig," said Mitchell. "His initial reaction to that suggestion was, 'Don't give me no pig valve.' Then, when they told him he could die, he changed his tune to, 'Give me the pig.'"

Robert was eventually turned around by the volunteer organization at Columbia-Presbyterian called "Gift of Life." They sent person after person into Robert's room in attempt to convince him that a Left-Ventricle Assist Device (L-VAD) was the best possible alternative for someone in his condition. All of these volunteers had undergone transplants and all of them appeared to be perfectly healthy. One man in particular who had undergone a transplant and then ran a marathon talked to Robert, and that helped calm his fears. "Talking to that man helped Robert come around," said Smith.

He finally agreed to the procedure, and on April 24, 1998, Oprah Winfrey's close friend, Dr. Mehmet Oz, the world-renowned transplant surgeon and now host of his own syndicated TV show, *The Dr. Oz Show*, performed the seven-hour operation. The L-VAD hardware Dr. Oz implanted inside Robert's chest was in fact a flat titanium cylinder measuring four inches in diameter and weighing about two and a half pounds. Connected to this cylinder was a foot-long driveline cord that snaked down the inside of Robert's torso, exiting his body through a hole near his stomach. From there it attached to a battery-powered system controller that Robert would have to keep strapped to his side.

The operation was a success. Robert Dunn's life had been saved for now.

"Kitty showed up in my hospital room the next day," said Robert. "She had a new boyfriend, but she couldn't stop herself from seeing me when she found out I was sick. I was overjoyed that she was there. I stroked her hair as she leaned in close to feed me. She held liquids near my mouth so I could sip with a straw. She took my dirty underwear home and washed it. When my catheter was removed, she even guided my limp penis into an open bottle so I could urinate. I felt like a dying cow, getting milked for the last time. But she got me through my post-op recovery, and gave me reason to live. I even began fantasizing that she would leave this guy and come back to me. Then, just like that, she was gone and no longer taking my calls."

"I tried to be totally there for him after the L-VAD operation," Kitty recalled, "but it was difficult for me. The fact that I was seeing someone else made it difficult, but Robert would always be my best friend. Even though we had been through some rough times as husband and wife and couldn't live together, once we gave each other a little space it was fine. He became the man I knew and the man with whom I had love. That person had re-surfaced again. That's what you do with people you care for. You try to be by their side, and even though I was in a new long-term relationship, the man knew that my former husband was sick and needed my help. I told my boyfriend that there would be times when I needed to go with Robert to the doctor, or be with him in the hospital, and my boyfriend was secure enough to understand. There were times he even dropped me off so I could see Robert. And then he picked me up when my visit was finished. I was attentive to Robert during those times.

"But Robert was seeing someone else too, but she never went to see him in the hospital," said Kitty. "She was only back in the picture when he was feeling stronger. I figured, if she was going to be his significant other, then she's the one who should be in the picture, through the good times and the bad, not me. I knew how to step out of the picture. I knew how not to return calls. I'm not saying it was a good thing. But I needed to save myself too. When I withdraw, I withdraw. I don't return calls. You can't get me. That's how I am. I take care of me. I needed to let go, and I did."

Without Kitty, Robert reverted back to the one thing he knew best: work. "After he got his mechanical heart, I would watch him at work, in the office and in the courtroom, and I would tell him to go home," said Smith. "But he wouldn't listen. He would come to work dressed in a suit, make appearances in court. Once he had a great scare because he had left one of the batteries at home. He would get stuck in traffic, or be late for a bus, the kinds of things that happen to the rest of us all the time, and yet he was trying to experience all of those annoyances with a mechanical heart. He had lost weight. He was fighting to stay alive. But he always thought forward, always saying, 'I'm going to beat this.'"

CHAPTER TEN

The four months of physical pain Robert had endured with a mechanical heart in his body was suddenly nothing compared to the emotional price he thought he was now being asked to pay. The anger and rage that had fueled him throughout his life had to now make room for the overwhelming fear and anxiety that accompanied his loss of control.

"While I didn't necessarily think that the rage I had in me for years had caused me to be ill," he said, "I felt rage that my body had betrayed me, and rage that I had to now go through this Frankenstein experience in order to continue living. I was waiting for somebody else's heart, waiting for doctors to put another person's organ into my body. It was nothing I wanted to do, and it left me unbelievably fearful, which I automatically turned into anger and rage. I didn't immediately connect it back to my childhood, but these were the feelings that had always been with me, stalking me, near or at the surface. But now I was directing it all at me, like I had somehow brought this on myself."

There was another slight problem that Robert wasn't talking about—his virility, or more to the point, the very real prospect that he could lose it. His immune system had correctly recognized the L-VAD as a foreign entity, causing his antibodies to go on the attack. Doctors said the only way to get those antibodies back under control was to give him chemotherapy, the side effects of which included the further reduction of his immune system, the possibility of cancer in many forms, baldness, and sterility.

"Just wait a fucking minute," was what he said to his doctors. "I'm not in enough pain from the mechanical heart? Now you're telling me that in addition I'm going to be a bald-headed, cancer-stricken infertile man?"

They said, "These are the things that can happen."

He said, "I'll tell you what. None of these things are going to happen, because I ain't doing it. No chemo."

They said, "You don't understand. You have to take the chemo because you can't get a human heart in your condition. The antibodies must match up, and if they are not under control, they will kill any heart we put in you. You have no choice."

He said, 'Yes, I do, and I'm not doing it."

His immunologist, Dr. Silviu Itescu, spent days and nights on the Internet and came back to him a week later and said that if they gave him testosterone, along with the chemo, it would arrest the production of his sperm and render it dormant during chemo. He said the chemo can't kill what isn't out there to be destroyed. It didn't allay all Robert's fears, but since it meant that he might be able to avoid sterility, he relented. The doctor said that under the circumstances he might want to increase the odds of having a child one day by establishing a relationship with a sperm bank

A sperm bank. The very idea made him furious. He was already angry at himself for being childless, and now his failed heart was forcing another indignity on him, "a twisted type of medical gymnastics," he said, "that held no guarantee I'd ever be a father. To me, a sperm bank was one more example of all this crazy white man's stuff. A sperm bank was not supposed to be for us. It wasn't manly, or virile. I always wanted to go in there like a man, and park myself inside a woman to create a kid. Not be handed a plastic container and an X-rated magazine by some pretty medical assistant who was pointing me to a room while leaving no doubt that she would not be coming in there with me. But I did take the doctor's advice and I booked an appointment at a sperm bank on Manhattan's East Side."

In the intervening days, Robert stayed in his mother's house in Staten Island. Going to work each day from Staten Island wasn't the easiest commute under any circumstances, waking up each day in his mother's condo, and then walking three blocks just to wait in line for the New York City bus that would drop him off at the Staten Island Ferry so he could get across the Hudson River and eventually to his law office near the World Trade Center.

As much as he loved and respected his mother, Robert surely would have preferred starting out each day in his own Midtown Manhattan apartment where he could wrestle with the relatively simple decision of whether to take the train downtown or drive to work in his new Mercedes.

Unfortunately, Robert's preferences and the realities of his life that summer had ceased to co-exist. He was a six-foot, four-inch, forty-three-year-old African-American who couldn't stand up straight without moaning in pain. He was staying at his mother's because it was no longer medically prudent for him to be alone. Certainly not with a mechanical heart implanted under his own failing heart, this "bridge to a human heart transplant," as his doctors had described it, which pressed against the inside of his ribs, limiting his every move, and forcing him to walk around, he'd say, "like a hunchback in a doll house," a man suddenly trapped by his own grotesqueness and the horrifying feeling that death could be imminent.

And of course it was the mechanical heart, and only the mechanical heart, that was keeping him alive.

But he tried to act normal, and each day he would sit uncomfortably on the crowded Staten Island bus alternately fiddling with a black leather briefcase wedged between his knees and fighting within himself not to judge the mostly white passengers who all seemed to be making an effort not to look at him.

With his suit jacket on, he might have given the appearance he was carrying a concealed weapon were it not for the strange sucking noise emanating from his body every time he took a breath, making it seem, at least to him, that the embarrassing gurgles from his insides were being projected throughout the bus on a loudspeaker.

In a post-Sept.11 world, the sight and sound of Robert Dunn on a New York City bus might have sent passengers scurrying for their own lives fearing the presence of a suicide bomber. But this was happening during the summer of 1998, three years before 9/11, when any large-scale terrorist attack on New York seemed almost unthinkable.

So the people around him just sat there for the most part reading their morning newspapers, listening to their favorite CDs, whispering on their cell phones, and doing just about anything to act oblivious to the large black man in their midst.

When the day for his sperm bank appointment finally arrived, Robert woke up at his mother's in Staten Island determined to drive himself into the city. He had been taking buses and hadn't been behind the wheel of his automobile since the L-VAD operation in April. Just the anticipation of driving again gave him a sense of power and freedom. The car represented independence, and he felt liberated just to be doing it again.

It was 11:30 a.m., and already dreadfully hot, the kind of humid mid-summer day that New Yorkers complain loudly about. With his mind bridling at images of plastic containers and porn magazines, he set his briefcase on top of his car, and fumbled for the car keys in his pocket. Settling into the front seat, he turned the air conditioner to full blast, and sped off. It felt great to be driving again.

At the toll booth for the Verrazano Bridge, which links Staten Island to Brooklyn, he reached into the back seat for his briefcase, which contained among many other items his wallet. But the briefcase wasn't there. With growing panic, he searched both seats in vain. Everything that mattered was in that briefcase, including even his spare computer pack, which was all that stood between himself and death if the L-VAD broke down.

Then he remembered placing the briefcase on the roof of his car. He hollered out to the toll booth attendant that he needed to make a U-turn. "I have a mechanical heart," he shouted, lifting his body and twisting it to show him the battery pack and driveline cord. "I'm sure he'd heard a lot of odd stories from motorists who were lost, broke, or in urgent need of a bathroom, but the look on his face told me he'd just heard a new one. He waved me through."

He sped frantically back to Staten Island, changing lanes without signaling, and the faster he drove, the more frightened he became. He thought, "What if my L-VAD froze while I was driving? What if I couldn't find the computer pack? I would die. And even if I survived, there would be no way for me to get back into my mother's house. She had already left for work, and the keys to her house were in my briefcase, under that damn computer pack."

Luckily, the L-VAD didn't malfunction. But when he reached his mother's house, the briefcase wasn't in the driveway. So he retraced his path on foot, walking along the Staten Island Expressway service road, searching under parked cars and kicking through the brush near the chain link fence that separated it from the expressway.

"There was too much ground for me to cover alone," he said, "so I knocked on a neighbor's door, and soon there were twenty people - adults and kids on bicycles - all of whom white, and all combing the road, looking for the missing briefcase. I was stunned by their kindness and caring. Not only did they help me search, they invited me into their homes, offering iced tea to quench my thirst and clean white towels to wipe the sweat from my face and neck. Back when I was a member of the Nation of Islam, I never even dreamed of crying in front of a white person. But here I was, defenseless and overcome with emotion, in front of a bunch of white people who responded to my pain with genuine compassion."

He never found the briefcase.

"I just sat there crying in Staten Island," said Robert. "I was filled with fear, hopelessness and pain, believing that God no longer loved me. I remember thinking that I couldn't take any more of this. I remember thinking that God had broken me, and maybe I wasn't supposed to make it."

Robert woke up the next morning wracked with nausea, which was followed immediately by crushing chest pain. The doctors had told him he couldn't possibly have a heart attack so long as he had the mechanical heart. But they were wrong. He was having a heart attack.

He was transported from Staten Island to Columbia-Presbyterian Hospital in an ambulance with a police escort. The L-VAD was all that was keeping him alive. Though his doctor reassured him that the heart attack would elevate his name on the heart transplant list, he lay in my hospital bed for the next five days, filled with terror, afraid to move.

"Two things kept me from going insane those few days," he said. "One was 'Conversations with God,' a tape narrated by Ed Asner in a voice so soothing that I thought, 'Okay, maybe I still can have a relationship with God.' The other was the Yankees. I felt as long as the Yankees were playing—and winning—everything must be all right with the world."

On July 29, he was well enough to go home. No one could say if or when a new heart might become available, but he was given a beeper, just in case, with instructions to rush to the hospital if it ever went off. He called Kitty again, and again she didn't return my call.

"I longed to be with my ex-wife and wanted her by my side, waiting with me for the beeper to go off," he said. "Kitty had seen me through the initial L-VAD operation, and cared for me like a nurse. But now she was avoiding me at all cost. Perhaps I had broken her like I thought God had broken me. I never felt so alone in my life."

CHAPTER ELEVEN

Betty remembered the night Dorothy showed up in Nanuet again with her three young sons. She said she needed to escape her boyfriend's rage and violence, and Betty took them all in, just like she always did.

Dorothy remained in Nanuet for a few months, and then one day Betty came home to find the following note: "Mom, I'm going upstate. Will call when I get settled. Love, Dot." Months went by before Betty heard from Dorothy again. When she finally did call, she told Betty that she'd settled upstate in Sullivan County. Her married alcoholic boyfriend, she said, finally moved out on his wife, and into another house with ample room for her and the boys. He promised Dorothy that his drinking was now under control.

"I always tried to tell her that she deserved better," said Betty. "I would say,

'There are nicer people out there. Maybe you can find one.'

"And she'd say, 'Oh, mom, I don't believe in marriage.' And when Roseanne got married," said Betty, "Dot wouldn't even come to the wedding. But she seemed excited about her own life. She believed her life was turning around. We were all so happy for her."

Dorothy ultimately landed a job caring for seniors at a nursing home in Sullivan County. She worked the late shift. It was her first real job in years. The father of Dorothy's boyfriend needed a place to live, and so he moved into the house his son was sharing with Dorothy and her three younger sons. The father also had an old car, and since Dorothy had no car—or a license to drive—the father agreed to drive Dorothy to work each night and then pick her up in the early morning hours when her shift at the nursing home was over.

"Roseanne was taught how to drive," Betty recalled, "and we had a teacher to teach Billy to drive. Dorothy absolutely needed to learn how to drive because she had all those kids. I think reality was finally settling in and she was learning how to drive."

Unfortunately, it was not soon enough. Just before sunrise on August 20, 1998, Dorothy got into her boyfriend's father's car, on the passenger seat side. Her shift was over, and she was happy to be going home. The school year would be starting up soon, she thought. A few more weeks until the routine of making peanut butter-and-jelly sandwiches began in earnest. After a long night of working, sleep sounded real good to her now.

Neither Dorothy nor her boyfriend's father had any reason to believe they'd encounter traffic of any kind, or even another motorist, when they turned onto the same old country road they'd been driving on for weeks. At this pre-dawn hour, though, two carloads of young Hassidic Jewish men just happened to be drag racing on that same country road, and both cars were going at a high rate of speed when they slammed broadside into Dorothy's car, directly on her side. Her boyfriend's father was hurt badly, as were a few of the Hassidic boys, but Dorothy's injuries appeared most severe. She was airlifted to Westchester Medical Center where it was determined she was brain dead. She was put on life support.

Betty Levigne rushed to the hospital with Billy Moore and Roseanne where they were given the sad news that Dorothy would never regain consciousness. She lingered for a few days on life support until someone from the hospital suggested pulling the plug and donating Dorothy's organs. Billy, her blood relative, was the only family member present who could sign the necessary papers, and he did so willingly.

It was August 23, 1998, and the beeper hadn't yet made a sound. After work that day, when Robert drove his car into the parking lot near his midtown apartment, the attendant, whom Robert barely knew, said, "I want you to know that Jesus came to me last night. And Jesus said, 'Tell the man that I have his heart for him. But tell him he must always remember where it came from, and tell him to tell others about the miracle I performed for him.'

"So," the man said, "you have your heart."

Robert was dumbfounded. It was late in the afternoon and he didn't know what to make of this. So he thanked the man for caring so much about him and he went upstairs to retire for the evening.

"I didn't have the strength to do anything else," he said. "Then, at eight o'clock on the morning of August 24, my beeper went off. I called the nurse practitioner at Columbia-Presbyterian, and she said, 'Robert, we have your heart. Come in." As frightened as I was about undergoing an actual transplant, I was buoyed by the words of the parking lot attendant and the praying he did for me."

Of course, Robert had absolutely no idea that at that very moment surgeons at Westchester County Medical Center were busily harvesting another human heart and packing it in an airtight traveling container, so it could be sent down to Dr. Oz and his surgical team at Columbia-Presbyterian.

Oliver Smith was in court when Robert called with news about a heart being found. "You could hear the worry in his voice," said Smith. "But he had complete faith in Dr. Oz."

The actual heart transplant, which under normal conditions would take nearly five hours to complete, took nine hours in Robert's case because of the scar tissue that had formed around his mechanical heart, and the delicate way it had to be cut out.

When he awoke on the morning of August 25, Dr. Oz was there to tell him that the operation had been a complete success. He said the heart they found was a perfect statistical match. A little later in the day another covering doctor came in, and he said, "Mr. Dunn, I'm only prepared to tell you three things about your donor—sex, age, and where the heart came from. Do you want to know?"

Robert said yes. The doctor said, "Female, forties, Westchester Medical Center, in Valhalla." Then he added that the heart had been out of body for less than two hours.

Robert couldn't get past the word "female." "Don't get me wrong," he told the doctor. "It's not like I don't appreciate getting any heart, but a woman's heart? In my body? I know my weight is down, but I'm normally 220. Was she that big?"

The doctor said no, she wasn't a large woman, and moreover that her heart would grow as Robert became healthier. Robert said he would have preferred the heart of a 25-year-old football player in prime condition. To which the doctor replied, "Just to let you know, you don't know a damn thing of what you're talking about. One, a woman's heart on average is ten years younger than a man of the same age. Two, this particular woman had no history of heart disease. Three, she had not reached menopause, and was still strong, still producing estrogen. Got any other problems?"

Robert did have other issues, but he was not going to continue the discussion with the doctor. But still, a woman's heart? He couldn't get over it—Robert Dunn, this macho guy who didn't even want a transplant or a mechanical heart with a woman's heart inside his body. He complained to his sister Sharon about the woman's apparent age—over forty, like *old*. In fact, others at Columbia Presbyterian who had received hearts at relatively the same time that Robert got his were all transplanted with much younger hearts, mostly from people in their twenties. Within a few months, though, every one of those other transplant recipients either rejected their hearts, or suffered some sort of complication. He was the only one of the group who experienced no setbacks at all.

"I figured this must have been some woman," he said. "I needed to know more about her."

CHAPTER TWELVE

The transplant community has an established protocol when it comes to the donating and transplanting of organs: recipients aren't supposed to know donors, and donors' families aren't supposed to know where their loved one's organs went. Anonymity, therefore, is the touchstone of organ transplanting. Doctors have found over the years that it just works better that way.

But Robert couldn't stop thinking about it. If the donor was such a perfect statistical match, then surely they must have had a lot in common. He spoke to people in the transplant unit at Columbia-Presbyterian, and they said the best they could do was forward a letter to the donor's family. Whether the family answered it was purely their decision.

So Sharon and Robert each wrote letters, thanking people anonymously for the gift of life he had received. But neither of them ever heard a word back. He wrote a second letter, then a third, and still there was no response. Then, in September of 1999, during a volleyball game at an annual "Gift of Life" picnic for organ recipients, a social worker he knew from Columbia-Presbyterian remarked how fit he had become. Indeed, his weight was back up by then. He was standing tall, and feeling very alive.

"You look fantastic," she said.

He said, "I must have a hell of a heart."

She asked him how much I knew about his donor, and he said not much: female, forties, Westchester Medical Center, in Valhalla. She said, "Stop by my office. I'll see if I can get her exact age."

Robert went to the woman's office the following week, and she did have the donor's age: forty-one. But she also had additional information, and it was like nothing he could have expected. After revealing the person's age, the social worker said, rather matter-of-factly, "White, Irish-Catholic."

Robert was completely blown away. "Although I no longer viewed the world from the contorted black-white prism of my youth," he said, "I couldn't believe it—a perfect genetic match, me and a white woman. Suddenly I wasn't so sure I wanted to find the donor's family. In the back of my mind, I feared they would reject me. I wondered how they might feel about a black person getting their loved one's heart. And beyond that, this particular black person—me, with my history of tremendous racial anger, this person who was nobody's saint. I feared—like I feared all my life—that I was not going to measure up. I didn't want to be a disappointment to them. I was afraid if they ever met me, they may start to think they made the wrong decision.

I know I judge myself too harshly," he said. "Always have. But I became really apprehensive about finding these people, and I let another four years go by before I did anything else about it."

In the interim, though, he tried to use his gift of life as motivation to help others. Many, many people prayed for him during his ordeal and he responded by offering his testimony at their churches throughout the New York metropolitan area. He talked about his renewed faith in God, and how he had become a more spiritual, gentler, and forgiving man after receiving his new heart. He used his law practice to act as guardian and court evaluator to many aged, sick, and incapacitated people, under Article 81 of the New York State Mental Hygiene Law. He helped seniors move residences. He delivered food to them, took care of their legal papers, and even tried to carry out their last wishes.

But something was missing. A white woman's heart was beating inside his chest, and the time had finally come for him to know more about it.

That's when I stepped in and offered to help Robert find his donor. He told me everything about her, which wasn't much: just the date of the transplant, the name of the hospital in Valhalla, and the belief that the donor was a 41-year-old white Irish-Catholic woman.

In just a few short days, I came back to Robert with an obituary I found in a local newspaper from Rockland County, a suburban New York community above Westchester and across the Tappan Zee Bridge. According to the obituary, the woman, Dorothy Moore, died on August 24, 1998, from wounds she sustained in an automobile accident. The story said she died at Westchester Medical Center, and listed her age at forty-one. Among the next of kin mentioned were a mother, Betty Levigne; a sister, Roseanne Mercado, a brother, Billy Moore, and five children.

My subsequent call to Roseanne Mercado confirmed that permission had been granted for Dorothy's organs to be donated. Roseanne even recalled the family receiving two letters, one from a Robert Dunn and another from his sister Sharon. It was clear in that moment that my friend Robert was living with Dorothy Moore's heart inside his body.

I asked Roseanne whether the family might want to meet Robert. She said she first wanted to talk to her mother, but she was certain there would be a positive response. I then told her that Robert was black.

"Oh, that's wonderful," Roseanne said. "Dot would have loved that."

When I phoned Robert afterwards to tell him of my conversation with Roseanne, he broke down and wept like a baby. "I knew I felt love for this anonymous person whose heart had given me life," he said. "But the thought that she might have loved the idea that her heart had gone to a man of color was practically too much for me to comprehend. A white Irish-Catholic, I thought. Where I come from, that is definitely not supposed to happen."

But it did. Without saying it, Roseanne seemed to indicate how right it was that a black person had her sister's heart. And when Robert visited the family some weeks later, he began to understand why.

He was invited to meet the family at Betty Levigne's ranch house in Nanuet, New York, a mostly blue-collar community in Rockland County. Although the house was small and cramped by almost anyone's standards, Robert felt the warmth the minute he walked in. Betty, in her 70s and widowed, was working as a custodian for the Nanuet public school system. Dorothy's younger brother Billy Moore, 47, was still living at home with Betty, and he was working as a janitor at the same public school. Roseanne was living a few blocks away in a house not much larger than her mother's, but she had managed to raise five children there with her husband, Ephram Mercado.

Robert sat in the same kitchen where Dorothy Moore ate as a child. Other relatives seemed to come from out of nowhere to meet him. He was greeted with hugs and kisses. They took pictures with him and openly prayed for him to live with Dorothy's heart forever.

"I never felt so surrounded by love, unconditional love," he said. "I held my hand to my heart, and through my tears I told these people that I could even feel Dorothy loving me, right at that moment.

Before I met these people," he said, "I felt embarrassed and ashamed that I hadn't changed much since I got a new heart and received the gift of life. In many ways, I was still clinging to the life I had always known: the angry lawyer and unworthy man, desperate to hold on to my virility and doomed to failure unless I could somehow have a child. Then I met this family, and you would have thought it was someone in my family who gave a heart to one of their loved ones, and not the other way around. That is how they treated me."

A few months later, Robert drove up to Nanuet again, this time to Roseanne's house. It was a day the two families had been planning since the fall. Robert's mother came with him, along with his sister Sharon, her daughter India, Robert's Aunt June, and his ex-wife Kitty. It was like a belated Christmas.

Betty was there, of course, along with Billy Moore, other nieces and nephews, all of Roseanne's children, and her husband Ephram, who also spent his formative years at St. Agatha's orphanage. They showered Robert with gifts, and had gifts for each member of his family. They constructed a family tree, and hung Robert's picture from one of the branches.

"They made me feel," he said, "like we were all one big family."

They told Robert that Dorothy's oldest son, Willie, would be visiting his relatives in Nanuet in May. Willie had been told everything about Robert, and he seemed as anxious to meet Robert as he was to meet him. There was little information available about Dorothy's daughter Elizabeth, and her three other sons, Allan, John and Jesse, were all taken from their father and adopted into different families shortly after the death of their mother.

"Willie, at least, would be a start," said Robert. "With Dorothy not here to do for her children as I would want to do for her because of what she'd done for me, I figured that at the very least I could try standing in her shoes, and maybe do something for Willie in her place.

"Did this mean that I would inherit Dorothy's children and in the process fulfill my own desires to be a father? Not likely," he said. "But I did feel like I was becoming a better man. When I was at Roseanne's house, enveloped in all that love and acceptance, I finally felt that, yes, I am worth it. But when Roseanne told me how she felt about me as a person, I automatically responded, 'You are all so good. I'm sure you'd feel this way about anybody.'"

And she said, "No, Robert. It's you. You are such a wonderful person. The idea that we could have helped in some way is the gift to us."

"I felt so loved," he said. "And this was the feeling I wanted my whole life. Because of how they accepted me, it was finally okay for me to accept myself. I couldn't wait to meet Willie. I just knew how important he was to my journey."

They ultimately met in Nanuet, on a Sunday in May. It was Mother's Day, a day that Robert would normally spend with his own mother. But she understood that her son needed to be in Nanuet that day, celebrating the holiday with Betty Levigne and her family, and especially with Willie, who had traveled up from Florida with his wife and three children.

Willie and Robert got along immediately, almost like they had known each other for years. They were each about to celebrate a birthday. Willie turning twenty-five on May 25, and Robert would be 50 two days later. A well-built man of medium height, Willie had a pencil-thin mustache, close-cropped dark hair, and an infinite amount of patience with his children, the youngest of whom, a son, was severely handicapped, wheelchair-bound, and unable to speak.

But Willie had no trouble speaking, and he told Robert in great detail about the suffering his mother did at the hands of her abusive boyfriend. "I could feel the anger welling up in me as Willie talked," said Robert. "Just point me in the direction of this abuser, I thought, and I'll kill him myself."

Willie had no knowledge of the man's whereabouts. But Robert knew it wouldn't be too difficult to find him. He had been arrested numerous times, for domestic violence, and parole violations.

"I thought, if only I could have been there to protect her, the way she had been protecting me. But at least I could protect her now," said Robert, "along with her spirit, and maybe in the process even her children."

Willie said that when his grandmother told him of Robert's existence, he considered it an act of God. "I always believed my mother had the biggest heart in the world," said Willie. "I know that if she could have ripped it out herself to give to someone else, she would have done that. I'm not surprised that my mother's heart turned out to be such a perfect match. It's as if the man upstairs knew that my mother lived a living hell every single day. She had to have a mighty strong heart to survive the way she did, especially under the circumstances of her life. Through it all, though, she always kept her composure, and she always tried to make life easier for those around her. They say that everything happens for a reason, and if God didn't want her living on earth anymore, living that horror and hell, He must have said, 'Come with me. You'll be safe, and you'll live in somebody else. And I have the perfect somebody picked out for you.' That's really how I feel."

After Robert and Willie finished talking and eating the food that Betty and Roseanne had prepared, Willie asked him whether he wanted to accompany him to his mother's grave. Willie hadn't been to the cemetery since his mother's burial in 1998, and here it was Mother's Day and he wanted to leave his mother a bouquet of flowers.

"When we arrived there," said Robert, "and I saw her name, Dorothy Moore, on the headstone, with a date of birth and a date of death, a date that corresponded to the day I received her heart, I began for the first time to see beyond my own good fortune of having been given another chance at life. When Willie kneeled down beside his mother's stone and cried over his mother's loss, I realized that there was another emotional component to my transplant, a certain kind of pain I had thus far been able to avoid. I may have been blessed, but others close to Dorothy Moore had been devastated by her loss. It was a feeling I had not previously considered, and suddenly I was crying too."

Two days later, Willie Moore along with his wife, children and other family members were taken by Robert to one of his favorite Chinese restaurants, a short walk from his downtown office on Maiden Lane. "He picked the restaurant, a very classy place," said Willie. "He said he went there a lot with clients. The owners and the help all seemed to know him.

"We talked almost immediately about how close we felt towards each other," said Willie. "Even though I had only met him days before, I felt like I knew him a long time. He spent a couple of hours with us, and he insisted on picking up the check. We were six people, he was one person, but he refused to let us pay. The bill was outrageous, definitely over $200. He wouldn't even let us leave a tip."

On the way back to Robert's office, he talked with Willie about getting together soon in Florida, and maybe even going deep-sea fishing together. "He wanted to see where I lived, how I lived, what my workplace was like," said Willie. "We talked a lot about my mom and how grateful he was to have her heart, which he said was as close to a perfect match, especially for a Caucasian and an African-American. 'On the dial for matches,' he said, 'you can't find better numbers.'"

The following day, Robert phoned his sister Sharon to tell her that his connection to Dorothy had been deepened by his new relationship with her son. Robert now felt attached to Dorothy in another way, and he knew he had to keep her heart at all cost.

"The feeling I had for her seemed to be coming from the depth of my soul," he said. "In a very short time I had grown to love the people in her family, but this was different. I had told her family once that I could feel Dorothy loving me. But now I could feel myself loving her. It was as if I was falling in love with her, and the feeling was as overwhelming as it was comforting."

But the feelings of love soon gave way to a melancholy, the

likes of which he had never known. No matter how much he tried to shake this new feeling, the worse it became. He knew he had everything to live for, but he felt himself fighting depression. "Was my graveside visit a mistake?" he asked. "Had I gotten too close? Was I suddenly taking on everyone else's pain? Was this why doctors preferred keeping the names of transplant donors anonymous?"

And more to the point was this sudden and extreme pain in his abdomen psychosomatic? Or was something much worse going on inside Robert Dunn? He couldn't sort it out. He was losing control, and I knew he needed help. So he called the one person in his life he counted on above all others—his sister Sharon.

It was almost midnight on Thursday, May 19, when he made the call. Sharon knew immediately that her brother was feeling low, and she tried to keep the conversation upbeat, telling him all about her plans to fly to Rome the next day. Sharon is a flight attendant for American Airlines, and she is always jetting off to some exotic land. Sharon had her own health problems, having successfully beaten stomach cancer, so Robert tried to focus on her. But it only worked for a little while, and pretty soon he was telling her about his own fears, especially as they related to the pains in his stomach.

"As a heart recipient," he said, "I had dealt with the issue of rejection numerous times since my operation in 1998. No matter what I was feeling for Dorothy, my body reacted to her heart as a foreign object, an unwelcome intruder. That is an entirely appropriate reaction, by the way, and when antibodies go on the attack, as they often do, rejection can occur. In my case, whenever that happened, doctors were always able to fine-tune my medication, and the rejection episode ceased in a matter of days.

"But the stomach pains this time reminded me of the nausea

I felt right before my heart attack in '98," he said, "the one doctors said I couldn't have with the L-VAD implanted under my own heart. I told Sharon that maybe my problem had become coronary in nature, and not simply another rejection. But what she really wanted to do was lift my sagging spirits, and so she brought up some of my prior rejections, and how the proper use to medication always helped. We ended the conversation with her telling me that she was leaving for Rome at 5 p.m., the following day.

"I'll be around for most of the day," she said, "if you need me."

Robert passed out in court the following morning. By the time the ambulance arrived, he was conscious again, and he started making calls on his cell phone, lying flat on his back as the ambulance made its way uptown to Columbia-Presbyterian, which over the years had become almost like Robert Dunn's second home.

It took him a long time to finally reach his sister. "Whenever I feel really afraid," he said, "I become feisty and agitated and not very polite. I think I started yelling at Sharon as soon as she picked up. I said, 'You have nine fucking phones in your house and in your pocketbook, and you don't answer any of them.' I said I had been desperate to reach her. I told her where I was, where I was on my way to, and how pissed off I was that I might have to spend my fiftieth birthday in the hospital."

The paramedics were mad that he was even on a cell phone, much less yelling into it and reacting with anger to the person on the other end of the line. But he shut them up by telling them to not even bother dropping him off in the emergency room, which at Columbia-Presbyterian often resembles something out of "M.A.S.H." Instead, Robert wanted to be left off across the street from the ER, in front of his doctor's office. Surely his cardiologist Dr. Donna Mancini would know what to do with him.

Just as Sharon was telling him that she would call Dr. Mancini, to at least tell her that her brother was coming, Robert started reacting like his chest pains had gotten worse. "The paramedics wanted him off the phone right then," said Sharon Dunn. "But before he hung up he made me promise that I would instruct the doctors to do whatever it took to keep him alive."

EPILOGUE

Sharon Dunn called her superiors at American Airlines to say she would not be making her scheduled flight to Rome, and immediately drove back to Staten Island to pick up her mother. The Dunn family had been dealing with Robert's health issues for so long that these kinds of frantic trips to the hospital were almost commonplace. But all Sharon really knew at that point was that the ambulance carrying her brother had arrived at Columbia-Presbyterian before their call disconnected. What she didn't know was that a resident in the ER had already determined that Robert was in the throes of an acute myocardial infarction, medical terminology for a heart attack. Dorothy Moore's heart, which had served Robert so well for nearly seven years, was failing.

Dr. Mancini had been functioning as Robert's cardiologist since the year after his transplant, and when she arrived at the hospital's cardial catheterization lab, her patient was unconscious and in full cardiac arrest.

"We resuscitated him in the cath lab," Dr. Mancini said, "and he was found to have occlusion of several arteries. He underwent emergency angioplasty with stent placement, but remained very unstable."

A second cardiac arrest occurred, followed by a third. "The whole time he was in the cath lab he was really tenuous, back and forth between ventricular arrhythmia, hypertension," said Dr. Mancini. "Basically, he was in and out."

After the third arrest, other doctors in the ER concluded that Robert was gone, but Mancini insisted on continued attempts at resuscitation. Incredibly, the attempts worked. He was barely alive, but alive. What Mancini and her team needed mostly now was time, time for Robert's extraordinary determination and will to live to take over, and time for Dorothy Moore's heart to rest.

"While he was having the arrests," Dr. Mancini said, "we were trying to decide whether we could get him stable enough to implant another mechanical heart. Once we did get him back, the consensus was to put off surgery for the time being and instead attach him to a heart-lung machine, induce a coma, and have the machine do the work of his organs until the next decision had to be made."

Family and friends soon took over an entire waiting room on the hospital's fourth floor. Betty Levigne and the extended family of Dorothy Moore lit candles and offered prayers in their churches and from their homes. Dorothy's son, Willie Moore, called Columbia-Presbyterian from his home in Florida and asked to speak with anyone in Robert Dunn' room. The operator told him that calls could only be accepted by members of the immediate family.

"Robert Dunn is my father," said Willie, who could have just as easily added, "my father, and my mother too."

Robert's ex-wife Kitty took Willie's call and told him there was little else to do now but pray. "So I started praying," said Willie. "I had everyone in my family praying."

The issue of how prayer affects life-and-death medical situations is a subject that will probably be debated forever, but in this case the prayers must have counted for something because by morning Dorothy's heart, which was spared from any strenuous work once the heart-lung machine was activated, was suddenly showing signs of becoming stronger.

By Saturday afternoon, May 21, Robert's cardiac output had improved enough for him to be slowly brought out of the induced coma. "It takes a while when you stop that kind of heavy sedation," Dr. Mancini said. "Several hours, in fact, for it to wear off. By Sunday morning, Robert was able to follow commands and hear my voice.

"I said to him, 'Robert, you have had an extensive MI. This heart is not working. The only way for you to survive is to get you re-transplanted,' which meant introducing another Left-

Ventricle Assist Device, the L-VAD. But I told him that because he was doing so poorly we would probably have to implant a V-VAD, which does the work of both the left side and the right side.

"Initially," she said, "he gave me a look, like, 'I can't do it.' But then he consented."

Sharon Dunn remembers her brother's reaction differently. "The doctor was not in the room when my mother and I walked in," recalled Sharon. "Bobby was conscious, but his mouth was filled with tubes, and he couldn't speak. I said to him, 'Bobby, they want to put in another mechanical heart. How do you feel about that?' He started pounding the bed with his hand, grunting, 'No, no no!' He did not want to go through that kind of operation again. He did not want to give up Dorothy's heart, and he knew that another mechanical heart meant the end of her heart."

Dr. Mancini never saw Robert banging on the bed, and never knew the extent of his protests. "Had he been telling me, 'No, no, no!' I wouldn't have done it," she said. "Another doctor was there with me that Sunday, and we both felt that Robert knew what we were talking about. He demonstrated that he wanted to go forward after he woke up."

Even Robert's transplant surgeon, Dr. Mehmet Oz, who had been consulting regularly with Dr. Mancini from the moment Robert was brought in to the ER that Friday, agreed that another operation was his only chance.

The Dunn family ultimately concurred with the medical team. The pledge Sharon made to her brother—to instruct the doctors to do whatever it took to save Robert's life—outweighed his own hesitation. Everyone involved was now on the same page. Everyone, that is, except Robert. In strict medical terms, he had consented to the V-VAD procedure, and he was soon induced back into a pre-op coma. But in his heart, "No, no, no!" really meant, "No, no no!"

The surgery was performed later that day as a matter of sound medical course, and although Robert somehow made it through the complicated five-hour operation, he never regained consciousness. His death was officially noted as Tuesday, May 24, 2005, but they could have easily counted back two days, to the moment when he pounded his hospital bed and grunted his answer loud and clear. Dorothy Moore had protected him for nearly seven years, and now it was his turn to protect her. And if that meant he had to sacrifice his own life in the process, well, that's how it was all supposed to turn out. Robert Dunn knew he could never repay Dorothy Moore anyway. She gave him the best seven years of his life. His change of heart was now complete, and she would remain in his heart forever.

ACKNOWLEDGEMENTS

I may have written this book by myself, but I never could have made it this far without proper access to the stories lived by the book's two real-life leading characters, Robert Dunn and Dorothy Moore. Dorothy didn't live long enough to know that her organs might one day be used to save another's life, but knowing what I know about her now, had the question been posed to her during her lifetime, she probably would have agreed to it without even the slightest hesitation.

Robert Dunn I did know, thanks to John Gibson's introduction, but I had no idea the full impact Robert would have on my life when we sat for the first time and had a cup of coffee in midtown Manhattan. He wanted very much to write this book with me, and although his time on this earth was cut short, I'd like to think that somewhere out there—or better yet, *in here*—he knows that the chronicling of his story made me a better man.

I want to thank the respective families of these two extraordinary people—specifically, Robert's mother, Dolores Monteiro, and especially his sister, Sharon Dunn, along with Dorothy's mother, Betty Levigne, Dorothy's sister, Roseanne Mercado, Dorothy's brother, Billy Moore, and her son, Willie Moore—for their unflagging confidence in me, and the help they provided me during what must have seemed to them to be an usually long process.

To that end, I also want to thank Paul Burt and his staff at Open Book for their support and patience, along with my agent Sharlene Martin.

And lastly, I want to thank my wife, Lois Mathias, and our two sons, Jesse and Brian Fink, for putting up with me and loving me unconditionally.

About the Author

Mitchell Fink is a celebrated journalist and writer best known for his three decades of breaking stories at the *New York Daily News, People magazine,* the *Los Angeles Herald Examiner,* CNN, Fox and CBS. He is also the author of *The Last Days of Dead Celebrities* and the co-author of the *New York Times* bestselling book, *Never Forget: An Oral History of September 11, 2001.*

Fink became like a brother to Robert Dunn during last two years of his life, absorbing his journey, from his childhood experiences of racism to his membership in the Nation of Islam and its world of black supremacy and beyond through college and law school, and eventually to the crushing realization that the enemy all along was the enemy within. He spent more than a year with Dorothy's family, chronicling her story.

Lightning Source UK Ltd.
Milton Keynes UK
UKOW04f0658181213

223244UK00004B/449/P

9 780985 273712